MILITARY'S
STRANGEST
CAMPAIGNS &
CHARACTERS

MILITARY'S STRANGEST CAMPAIGNS & CHARACTERS

Extraordinary but true stories from over
two thousand years of military history

Tom Quinn

PORTICO

To PJ and SJ

Acknowledgements

Thanks for suggestions, old books, goose down, tea and battle plans to Katy, Alex, James, the game show experts in Chiswick, Gabrielle Koonin, Charlotte Wadham, Richard Tarlton, William Kempe and Jane Donovan.

First published in Great Britain in 2006

This edition published in 2010 by
Portico
10 Southcombe Street
London
W14 0RA

An imprint of Anova Books Company Ltd.

ISBN 9781907554131

A CIP catalogue record for this book is available from the British Library.

10 9 8 7 6 5 4

Printed and bound by Bell and Bain Ltd, Scotland

This book can be ordered direct from the publisher at www.anovabooks.com

Contents

Introduction

'Only the dead have seen the end of war' – Plato

Military history is full of strange stories – stories of extraordinary coincidences, of survival against all the odds, of strange meetings, eccentric characters, madmen, heroes and villains.

The sheer facts of warfare are themselves often bizarre – take the fact that in World War One more than one hundred thousand pigeons served their country. And in other conflicts elephants, camels, cats, canaries and even glowworms have been used, the latter highly effective in throwing just enough light to read a map by. But the antics of animals are as nothing to the mad, bad and incomprehensible antics of the millions of humans who have taken part, sometimes nobly sometimes ignominiously, in war and it is the strangest of their tales that, for the first time, are gathered here.

A disproportionate number of tales may seem to come from one or two wars or periods: Wellington is strongly represented because, as one modern commentator succinctly put it, he was as mad as a balloon, but he was also an extraordinarily brilliant military commander. The First World War inevitably takes up many pages too, simply because it was a war that has produced a greater number of books, including, of course, poetry and memoirs, than any other in history.

But whatever your interest you will find it represented here, from ancient battles, through medieval and modern wars; from Europe, Asia and America, *The Military's Strangest Characters and Campaigns* brings together the most bizarre stories from more than two thousand years of warfare.

Tom Quinn
London, October 2005

MARATHON BATTLE

GREECE, 490 BC

In 490 BC a council of Athenian military officers met on a mountain overlooking the plain of Marathon on the eastern coast of Attica. They were trying to decide whether to attack an enemy encamped on the shore beneath them and though they didn't know it at the time, the result of their decision was to change the course of history.

There were ten generals, one for each of the local tribes into which the Athenians were divided. Each general led the men of his own tribe. The eleventh council member was the Polemarch or War-Ruler: he would lead the right wing of the army in battle. At Marathon Callimachus was the War-Ruler.

It is estimated that the eleven council members had command of about ten or eleven thousand well-trained and highly equipped fighting men and perhaps a similar number of irregular and less well-trained troops. The opposing Persian army camped down below on the shore, by contrast, consisted of more than one hundred thousand well-armed men – men who had arrived in a vast fleet of warships. The Persians were commanded by Datis and Artaphernes.

One extraordinary man is generally given the credit for victory in the Battle of Marathon, which is unquestionably one of the most extraordinary battles in military history. Miltiades (550–489 BC) was said to be descended from the legendary Achilles. It was his knowledge of the Persian armies, their training and weaponry that convinced him that the Greek troops were so much the superior fighting force that they would succeed even against the vast army facing them. Miltiades saw that the position of the Greek forces also gave them the huge advantage of being able to mount a sudden and devastating attack but it was a decision of enormous risk and daring. First he had to persuade the Council of War and after lengthy discussion the casting vote went to Callimachus, the War-Ruler, and the decision was made to attack.

The Persians actually made things easier for the Greeks because they had hesitated and delayed, hoping that the size of their army would intimidate the Athenians or that their spies and groups of partisans would somehow enable them to achieve victory without resorting to full-scale battle. It was a fateful tactic but given the difficulties of attacking a force in a stronghold above them, it is perhaps not impossible to see why the Persians were uncharacteristically hesitant. We only know it was September 490 BC when battle commenced.

Callimachus led the right wing; the Plataeans formed the extreme left; Themistocles and Aristides commanded the centre. The line consisted of heavily-armed spearmen who, breaking with tradition, moved forward at a run and in a hugely extended line to prevent the Persians outflanking them. The line was weakened by this but only at the centre, where Miltiades felt it would be easy to re-group; on the flanks the line was tight and well ordered. The idea of running was to ensure as far as possible that the deadly Persian cavalry did not have time to mount and organise themselves before the Greeks were upon them.

The historian Herodotus describes what happened next: 'When the Persians saw the Athenians running at them, without horse or bowmen, and in small numbers, they thought these were madmen rushing to certain destruction.' The Persian army – made up of men from Hyrcania and Afghanistan, from Khorassan and Ethiopia, from India, Iraq and Egypt – prepared to do battle, but they were effectively mercenaries with no racial or ethnic bonds, unlike the Greeks who had their national honour to defend.

Initially the Persians broke through the centre of the Greek line, but the flanks held and those who crossed the line were

2

destroyed or allowed to flee in disarray by the closing of the two outer flanks, which then attacked the centre force of the Persians. In close combat the Persians were simply no match for the Greeks, who fought in tightly packed formations and under great discipline. Had the Persians been able effectively to use their cavalry, things might have been very different but the moment came when the Persians' morale left them and the whole army began to crumble.

The hordes of Asia turned and fled to their ships, which the Greeks then attacked with fire. It is estimated that nearly seven thousand Persians died, while the Athenians are said to have lost just 192 men. Even allowing for exaggeration by the victors, it was a quite remarkable victory.

HUNGRY DEFEAT

GREECE, 405 BC

One of the most famous conflicts in the history of warfare, the thirty-year Peloponnesian War, ended simply because the Athenian army got hungry. The decisive defeat that gave Sparta its final crushing victory over Athens came in 405 BC at Aegospotami on the Hellespont.

After his success at the Battle of the Arginusae Islands some months earlier the Athenian commander took his huge flotilla of ships – the Athens Navy being the source of its power – to the small river mouth at Aegospotami. The Spartan fleet rode at anchor nearby, just across the Hellespont, but apparently in no mood for battle.

For four days the Athenian Commander Conon tried to tempt the Spartans to move their ships out into the Hellespont to do battle, but the Spartans refused to move, knowing that the Athenians were still the better trained and equipped for sea battles – Greek sea battles involved ships ramming each other and then close hand-to-hand fighting as the men boarded each other's vessels, or grappling devices were fitted, which hooked on to the enemy vessels, which were then unable to pull away.

Having failed to persuade or tempt the enemy to battle Conon made a strange, almost unfathomable decision that was to reverberate down through history. Most probably he had no choice, simply because food and drink for his army was running low, but he beached his ships and his men disappeared into the surrounding countryside to look for food. The Spartan leader Lysander had luckily sent out a couple of scouting ships to see what the enemy was up to. When they reported back that the Athenian ships had been beached, Lysander immediately launched an attack and all but nine of the Athenian ships were destroyed or captured. The nine who escaped returned to Athens, which was quickly besieged by the Spartans. Faced with a blockade and its fleet destroyed, the Athenians gave up. Their ancient democracy vanished forever when the city walls were torn down and the city made subject to Spartan rule.

WARS FOR BOARS

GREECE, 404 BC

Ancient battles must have been an extraordinary mix of practical weapons of war and weapons that, by modern standards, seem completely mad. Take pigs, for example. According to Pliny the Elder (died AD 79), pigs were the ultimate weapon should you have to fight an army using elephants and in the ancient world the elephant was the equivalent to the modern tank. According to him, only one thing could get the better of the elephant that is 'scared by the smallest squeal of a pig; and when wounded and frightened, they always give ground'.

In the Siege of Megara (now a suburb of Athens) during the Peloponnesian War (431–404 BC), legend has it that the Megarians beat back the attackers' elephants in a most cruel and bizarre way. They poured oil over dozens of pigs, set them alight and then set them loose against the elephants.

At Edessa in Macedonia a siege had reached the city walls and one elephant was so close to the defenders that it was virtually looking over the walls. The defenders pushed a squealing pig into the face of the elephant which apparently turned and fled.

ELEPHANTS AT WAR

ITALY, 218 BC

Like Scottish highland dress and the noise of the bagpipes, the elephant's real impact in war came from its appearance. Ancient writers again and again emphasise the terrifying sight of mounted elephants approaching over a hill, particularly for those people who had never seen or heard of the huge animals before. Those lucky enough to have elephants in their army knew how great a psychological impact they would have and they deliberately enhanced this by kitting their elephants out in bright, heavily armed cloths and shields.

One Roman chronicler records the defeat of an army of Britons: 'Caesar had one large elephant, which was equipped with armor and carried archers and slingers in its tower. When this unknown creature entered the river, the Britons and their horses fled and the Roman army crossed over'.

But of course the ancients knew very little about elephants; they were rather like the English animal keepers charged with looking after the first bear to reach England alive. Out of pure kindness they fed it bread and beer, and were baffled when it starved to death. Likewise it was assumed that because the elephant was big and armed with tusks it was naturally aggressive, but of course nothing could be further from the truth: elephants would much rather run than fight. Pliny the Elder records when Hannibal first realised that elephants were not warlike creatures:

Hannibal pitted a Roman prisoner against an elephant, and this man, having secured a promise of his freedom if he killed the animal, met it single-handed in the arena and much to the chagrin of the Carthaginians dispatched it. Hannibal realized that reports of this encounter would bring the animals into contempt, so he sent horsemen to kill the man as he was departing.

Perhaps the most famous military commander of elephants was Hannibal who, in 218 BC, crossed the Alps with nearly forty elephants and defeated the Romans at Trebbia. Here, the Romans largely ran in terror and their losses were heavy but like so many weapons of war, elephants soon became familiar and ways to defeat them were quickly developed – not least of course being the squealing pig.

Eventually it was realised that elephants were actually relatively easy to defeat and the Roman velites (lightly armed soldiers) were usually engaged to defeat them. They simply manoeuvred quickly and continually around the elephants on horseback, stabbing them with long lances until the weakened animals, which were too slow to fend off the cavalry attacks, collapsed and died.

FIRE TRICK

CHINA, AD 241

In the West we often forget that China was a sophisticated civilisation long before Greece and Rome and in warfare, as much as anywhere, the Chinese developed complex tactics that are still, even today, studied in military academies.

During the early part of the Christian era, a particularly turbulent period of Chinese history, the Generals Sun Pin and Tien Chi led the armies of the Chi state against the armies of Wei, the latter commanded by Pang Chuan. Sun Pin was a particularly astute military leader, who knew that his opponents believed the Chi state was inhabited entirely by cowards and its army was even worse: that it was, in short, composed of a bunch of fickle, useless and uncommitted soldiers who would desert at the first opportunity. But Sun Pin decided to use his own countrymen's reputation for cowardice among the enemy to his advantage . . .

As soon as Sun Pin's army had crossed into Wei territory they made camp on a raised area of ground and the General gave orders that a staggering one hundred thousand fires were to be lit as darkness fell. On the second night the huge army stayed on the same piece of ground but this time the General ordered that only fifty thousand fires were to be lit. Then, on the third day, the army was astonished when their general insisted they must remain where they were for a third night, only on this occasion they were to light just twenty thousand fires.

The commander of the Wei army, Pang Chuan, who was watching from the other side of the valley, is reported to have

9

said: 'I knew the army of Chi were cowards – so many have deserted that their numbers are already reduced by more than half.' Knowing that Pang Chuan would use this apparent weakness as an excuse to attack, Sun Pin began to retreat. Reaching a narrow pass in the mountains that he knew the opposing general would arrive at after dark that coming night, he ordered his men to strip the bark from a tree and on the bleached surface write the words: 'Pang Chuan shall die under this tree'.

As darkness fell, Sun Pin's huge army hid in the surrounding hills and waited. A party of his best archers was told to watch the tree and to fire as soon as they saw a light. Darkness came and Pang Chuan arrived at the tree, now vaguely discernible in the darkness. He ordered a light to be struck so that he could make out the indistinct marks on the tree and as soon as this occurred and at the very moment when he must have read the prophetic words he was killed by a volley of arrows. Without their leader the Wei army quickly dispersed.

ONE WOMAN ARMY

DENMARK, AD 850

During a three-year warring expedition along the coast of what was then known as Vinland – modern North America – the Viking Thornfinn Karlsefni's wife Freydis is said to have fallen pregnant.

While discussing a trade issue with the Vinlanders – ancestors of today's native Americans – an argument broke out and then a fight. The discussions had been taking place on a beach but, as they were heavily outnumbered the Vikings quickly retreated to their ships.

Freydis tripped and fell as she ran, and was left to fend for herself. She picked up a dropped sword and stood to face her attackers. Though heavily pregnant and alone, she screamed and ran at them. The Vinlanders were so astonished that they turned and fled.

THE CHILDREN'S CRUSADE

FRANCE, 1212

In the great history of strange military engagements, eccentric soldiers and mad old colonels, for utter foolishness and stupidity very little comes near the Children's Crusade. But that perhaps is to look at this strange medieval phenomenon from too modern a perspective for in medieval times children were not seen as being different from adults in the way that they are today. They were regarded far more as being adults in miniature: as capable of action or inaction, good deeds and bad, as adults.

The story of the Children's Crusade really starts with the failure of the Fourth Crusade. In 1202 thousands began the long trek from Europe to the Holy Land, but most vanished on the way, died from sickness or turned back long before they reached Jerusalem. According to some historians, those who survived spent more time plundering the villages and town through which they passed. Notably disinclined to go on a crusade themselves, the Pope and other Christian leaders were in despair at the failure of the Fourth Crusade since it was seen as a Christian duty to re-capture the Holy Land from what were then seen as infidels. So the Children's Crusade must have seemed like a godsend to bishops and cardinals who wanted action, at least from others.

In 1212, for reasons that have never entirely been explained, a group of French children set off for Jerusalem. The group was made up entirely of young children. They let it be known that they had no fear of the Muslim Army, who might slaughter them if they ever reached the Holy Land, nor had they any fear of being attacked on the way – God, they were convinced, would protect them. But of course nothing of the sort happened.

The Children's Crusade was led by a young French boy called Stephen of Cloyes – at the time he was just twelve, and had clearly convinced himself and everyone else that he was divinely inspired. A shepherd from a remote farm, he could neither read nor write, but he walked to the court of King Philip of France and announced that he had a letter from Christ, telling him it was time to recapture Jerusalem. The King dismissed the young crusader but Stephen, who today would have been treated in hospital, wandered the villages and towns of France telling everyone about his letter and his instructions from on high.

Like most divinely inspired people, Stephen made outlandish claims that were never likely to stack up. He said that any child who followed him to Jerusalem needn't worry about sailing across the Mediterranean as the water would simply part and allow them to walk all the way. Deranged he may have been, but by the summer of 1212 Stephen had persuaded more than thirty thousand children to follow him. Rather than trying to stop them, the Church hierarchy actively encouraged them to go.

The army of children set off across France, cheered at intervals along the route by adults convinced this crusade would succeed simply because it was divinely inspired – though of course they thought that about all the earlier crusades, too.

The Church never officially blessed the Children's Crusade, but they were happy to see it take place, if only because they hoped it would embarrass European kings and emperors into taking serious military action to recapture Jerusalem. Those of a religious cast of mind may, even today, be astonished to hear that the sea did not part to allow the children to cross. In fact, by the time the Crusade reached Marseilles their number was already seriously reduced – children had been kidnapped, some had died of exhaustion or malnutrition; others simply gave up.

Somehow the remaining children organised their passage by boat. After they left Marseilles nothing certain was ever heard about them again. We know they did not reach Jerusalem, and more than a decade later, reports filtered back from travellers in North Africa of sightings of pale-skinned adults in several villages. One priest reported that he'd spoken to some of these European-looking Africans and discovered they were the few survivors of the Children's Crusade. These survivors told him that when they left Marseilles all those years ago, two of their seven ships had sunk and all the children were drowned. The other five ships were captured by pirates and the children sold and dispersed.

But despite the utter failure of the first Children's Crusade, there was yet more to come. A smaller Children's Crusade set off from Germany in the same year: 1212. A young boy called Nicholas gathered together twenty thousand other children and young men and women (this time a fair number were young adults) and they set off across the Alps, where many died, either from exhaustion or the cold.

When the remaining party reached Italy they met the Pope who sensibly told them to go home. Some did, but others left Pisa by ship for Jerusalem and were never heard of again.

THE BATTLE OF CRÉCY

FRANCE, 1346

The Battle of Crécy is one of those astonishing military events that even now it is hard to believe really happened. In essence it involved an English army of roughly ten thousand men defeating a joint French and Genoese army of at least twenty-four thousand and, in so doing, Edward III's English army killed more of Philip VI's men than there were English soldiers.

Under Philip, the French army met the English (under Edward III) at the village of Crécy in northern France. A day earlier at Abbeville the French had already declined to fight, but Philip was so sure he would win, simply because his army so outnumbered the English army, that he made a list of the English knights he planned to take prisoner.

Philip's battle plan involved unnerving the English with an initial volley of arrows from his highly trained Genoese archers, but he had miscalculated: the Genose marched toward the English line but before they'd come within range of their crossbows, the English longbow men released a deadly salvo of arrows. The crossbow men retreated in panic and were cut down by French horsemen coming up behind them, outraged at what they saw as cowardice.

When Philip's horsemen came within range of the English longbow men they, too, came under a sustained and deadly attack. They turned to retreat and crashed into the cavalry, who were still charging forward. The resulting mass of confused and tangled men and their mounts made an easy target for those deadly English arrows. Despite their heavy losses the French

15

charges continued but after at least twenty failed attempts to break through the English lines, the horsemen's attacks became increasingly difficult as they had to be made over the bodies of thousands of dead and dying men and horses. When the battle had ended Philip's ally – the King of Bohemia – lay dead, along with more than twelve hundred knights and eleven princes.

Crécy was a battle that established England as a major military force and convinced generations of English soldiers of their innate superiority to all comers.

QUICK-THINKING SCOT

FRANCE, 1356

The best soldiers are those able to think as well as fight and a particularly brilliant, if rather bizarre bit of quick thinking, occurred after the Battle of Poitiers in 1356. We have to remember that at this period the Scots felt they had much more in common with the French than with the English, and accordingly many clan chiefs fought against the English at Poitiers. One such was Archibald Douglas who, kitted out in his finest armour and looking every inch the lord that he was, found himself captured by the French at the end of the day's fighting.

Knights and lords were almost always captured and then ransomed in medieval battles – a live knight was always worth more than a dead one – but this was by no means a certainty and Douglas must have been very worried indeed about his fate. But he was saved by the extraordinary actions of his kinsman, Sir William Ramsey of Colluthy, who had also been captured. As the French knights inspected their prisoners, Sir William saw his chance. He stared at Lord Douglas and pretended to fly into a rage, shouting at him: 'You cursed murderer! How do you come to be decked out in your master's armour? Come here and pull off my boots, you slave!'

Douglas immediately did as he was told, but probably wondering what on earth was going on. Having been handed his boot, Sir William immediately used it to beat Lord Douglas about the head, shouting and berating him. The French knights milling around assumed that battle weary and perhaps concussed Sir William had simply gone slightly mad. They immediately intervened and told Sir William that he had assaulted a great lord, though of course they had no idea who Lord Douglas was at this stage and were merely judging him by his magnificent armour.

'He is not a Lord,' Sir William is supposed to have told the French knights. 'He is a scullion, a slave, a no one who is wearing his master's clothes. I shouldn't wonder if he has killed him. Go, you villain, and find the body of my cousin, your master, and when you have found it, come back so that I may bury him decently.' Sir William then ransomed the supposed servant for forty shillings and kicked him out of the door. By now Douglas saw his chance and was long gone before the French nobles realised their mistake.

BOSWORTH

ENGLAND, 1485

Apart from being one of English history's most famous battles, Bosworth is remarkable for a number of other reasons. It has been said that it marked the end of the Middle Ages – or at least of medieval forms of warfare – as it involved, for example, the last ever charge of mounted knights and was the last battle in which an English king lost his life. The battle was also pivotal as it saw the end of the Plantagenet dynasty and the arrival of the mighty Tudors.

The events leading up to the Battle are pretty straightforward: the future Henry Tudor was an exile in Paris – he was actually Earl of Richmond at this time – but his claim to the English throne was a strong one. He sailed for England on 1 August 1485 to attempt to wrest the crown from Richard III, who had been king for only two years.

At Bosworth, Richard assembled his troops on Ambion Hill and took charge of the cavalry himself, his rear position being taken by the Earl of Northumberland. The Earl of Oxford was appointed to command the main portion of Henry's army since Henry had no military experience whatsoever – Gilbert Talbot took command of the right wing, Sir John Savage, the left. Henry and his followers joined Sir John Savage on the right, which meant the left wing was weak. But it was off to the left that Henry Stanley kept his troops slightly at a distance. Historians have argued ever since whether even at this early stage of the battle Henry knew that Stanley would support him. Some historians believe it was never a certainty that Stanley would come to Henry's aid, and that he only did so because he saw his chance to be on the winning side. If events had unfolded in a rather different way, Stanley might well have supported Richard.

Richard attacked first while Henry's troops were still moving into position. After an initial flurry of shots from cannon and numerous volleys of arrows from Richard's crack team, some eight thousand of Richard's men charged downhill towards the Earl of Oxford. Henry's archers fired on the charging army. After intense hand-to-hand fighting Richard's men were still unable to break through Henry's wedge shaped formation and the Royalists retreated back up Albion Hill. Some time later another similar attack also failed.

It was at this point that Henry, surrounded by his entourage of knights, rode across the battlefield towards Stanley, who had so far taken no part in the battle. Seeing this movement Richard and some one thousand of his knights charged down the hill, hoping to kill Henry – this was the last-ever charge of mounted knights in battle.

Henry's standard bearer was killed in the charge and Richard himself fought through the mass of struggling knights toward Henry. He might well have reached Henry as the future Tudor king was accompanied by relatively few knights, but then came the key moment when the battle's outcome was decided. Stanley and his men – who had so far taken no part in the battle – decided to attack the flank of Richard's army of one thousand knights. Sir William Stanley and his four thousand men tore through Richard's army, and what had been a potentially brilliant move by Richard turned into a disaster for him.

As the fighting intensified Richard lost his horse but continued to fight bravely on foot, surrounded by Henry and Stanley's men. It is said that Sir Percy Thirlwall, the King's standard bearer, was still holding Richard's banner aloft, despite having lost both his legs. Richard was eventually cut down – probably by a Welsh soldier and with a halberd. In the way of medieval battles his body was then stripped and mutilated.

Seeing their king killed the Royalist army fell apart and fled, and Henry mounted a small hill, where he was crowned. Legend has it that Richard's crown was found hanging in a thorn bush. Richard's naked body was displayed for two days in a local church before being buried in a plain tomb.

At the Reformation Richard's grave was desecrated and the King's bones thrown into the nearby river Soar. His tombstone was later used to make a watering trough before being broken up to create a path or some tavern steps (the story varies) – which is why Richard III is the only English king since 1066 not to have a permanent and accredited tomb. But then, on the other hand, no other king since Richard can claim to have died bravely in battle rather than sitting at home while others did the fighting.

GIANT CROSSBOW

ITALY, 1486

Most people think of Leonardo Da Vinci (1452–1519) as one of the greatest artists who ever lived. Certainly his Mona Lisa, now in the Louvre, is one of the most famous pictures in the world, but painting was actually only a small part of Leonardo's vast output. His dozens of volumes of notes and sketches – many of which are still unaccounted for – were at least as often devoted to military matters, fortifications and weapons, as to portraits and landscapes.

Leonardo drew plausible parachutes, a convincing helicopter and numerous plans for sling shots, battering rams, a primitive tank and giant catapults for hurling rocks over the battlements during sieges. In the service of the Borgias he was specifically employed to put his mind to practical military problems that required practical inventive solutions.

But Leonardo was prone to eccentric military creations and one of his most bizarre inventions was a gigantic crossbow. Drawings for the crossbow survive and the masses of jottings Leonardo made in his notebooks about the project reveal that for some time at least he really thought it might be made to work.

Building a giant crossbow – perhaps as much as forty feet long and thirty across – is not simply a matter of increasing the size of a normal crossbow. The stresses and strains are totally different and Leonardo realised this: his notes reveal ingenious methods for creating a laminated structure that would both bend and allow lateral movement, vital given the distance the projectile would have to be dragged back along the body of the crossbow before being released.

Leonardo's crossbow was not intended to fire arrows but rather large boulders or cannonballs. Since much of late medieval warfare in Italy was based on city states attacking each other the winner in any conflict was likely to be the side that could most effectively breach the enemy's defences. If Leonardo's gigantic crossbow had been made to work it would have hurled boulders at a city's wall with enough power to break through them.

An elaborately geared ratchet and pinion system was to be employed to load or draw back the bow and it was probably at this stage that there might have been misgivings about the practicality of actually using the thing. Given the probable dimensions the force necessary to get the bow ready to fire would have been enormous, possibly beyond the capabilities of the materials available then to build such a weapon. But Leonardo's crossbow is still a strange and wonderful idea and one that, with modern materials, could probably be built today.

THE BATTLE OF LEPANTO

GREECE, 1571

The Battle of Lepanto is one of history's most extraordinary battles for two main reasons. First, it was the last battle ever in which the two opposing sides used ships powered entirely by oarsmen and second, it was the defeat of the mighty Ottoman Empire at Lepanto that signalled the beginning of the end of that empire. Before Lepanto the Turks were considered invincible on land and sea but afterwards the spell was broken and the Turks were exposed as human and fallible after all.

The battle took place on 7 October 1571 at a place called Nafpaktos on the Gulf of Lepanto, a long strip of the Ionian Sea that separates the Greek mainland from the Peloponnesian Peninsular. On 5 October the great Turkish sea commander Ali Pasha left the harbour at Lepanto and moved westward. Pasha knew that enemy ships were approaching but the exact position of the Christian fleet was more difficult to determine, which is why he relied on signals from lookouts on the rocky hills along the coastline. With no certain news he decided that the main fleet – almost three hundred and fifty ships in total – should wait in a sheltered spot a dozen or so miles from the entrance to the Gulf of Patras.

When the forward ships sighted each other the Turks fired the first volley, which was immediately answered by a double volley from the commander of the Christian fleet, the Austrian Don Juan. Rowed ships were actually quicker and more manoeuvrable than one might imagine, but superior tactics and firepower saw early Austrian successes. Within an hour the continuous firing of the Austrian fleet had sunk more than a dozen Turkish ships and many others were severely disabled. After those initial successes the battle became a disaster for the Turks and by late afternoon almost every Turkish ship was sinking or at least badly damaged.

Don Juan's ships gathered at the northern end of the Gulf. More than twenty thousand of his men had been killed or injured but incredibly, only fifteen Christian ships had been lost. Nearly eighty thousand Turkish sailors had died with hardly a ship escaping.

Across Christian Europe the victory was celebrated for weeks on end. 7 October was declared a public holiday and Turkish invincibility was no more. Following the extraordinary battle, rowed galleys vanished forever, but it was extraordinary for another reason: the great Spanish writer Miguel de Cervantes was an unknown infantryman who was wounded at the battle but survived to write *Don Quixote*, one of world's greatest works of literature.

MYTHICAL BEAST

MEXICO, 1580

Despite their later extraordinary abilities as horsemen, the native inhabitants of the Americas had never seen a horse until the Spanish arrived hot on the heels of Columbus and in search of plunder. Indeed the horse so terrified the Indians, who assumed it was a demon from hell, that it helped cow them into submission in their tens of thousands. The Spanish, moving across the continent and destroying everything in their wake, knew the power of the horse and to sustain the myth of its unearthly powers they did everything they could to prevent a horse – live or dead – ever falling into the hands of the Indians.

At first this was easy while the Spanish achieved continuous victories over the native people but the moment came when a Tlascalan army broke through the Spanish infantry and reached their mounted soldiers. One of the cavalrymen was quickly pulled to the ground and killed, and his horse was then slaughtered by an enraged group of Tlascalans. But the Spanish were so concerned that the mystical animal would lose its power that they fought with renewed strength over the body of the dead horse. On this occasion the Indians were victorious and they carried off the horse's body. They apparently cut it into pieces, which were then sent to the various centres of population in the Tlascalan region to show the people that the fabled mythical beast was, in fact, simply a large four-legged animal that could be killed.

The commander of Spanish troops in the area ordered thereafter that all horses killed in battle must be buried.

HARD CASE

ENGLAND, 1646

As a young man Richard Steele, who founded the original *Spectator* magazine in the early eighteenth century, had been a soldier in the lifeguards. He joined after leaving university and during his time heard many tales of army life. His favourite – which he always insisted was true – concerned a man who'd served in the Civil War (1642–9).

During a skirmish the soldier had been captured by the enemy – the Civil War was such a bloody and brutal business that captives were usually given pretty short shrift and executed. The soldier was duly condemned to be hanged, but the sentence was to be carried out on the Friday, and on the Thursday the soldier was allowed to write one last letter to his wife. He knew that his wife would not receive the letter until after his death and taking account of this, he wrote as follows:

Dear wife
Hoping you are in good health as I am at this present writing. This is to let you know that yesterday between the hours of eleven and twelve I was hanged, drawn and quartered. I died very penitently and every body thought my case very hard.

As luck would have it the man sent the letter and on the morning of his execution he was rescued by a group of his own soldiers. Instead of dying he saw those who had condemned him taken to the scaffold. But before he'd had time to write again to his wife and tell her that he had not in fact died, he discovered that she had already re-married. However, he didn't make a fuss, knowing – as he told anyone who would listen – that she had the proof that he was dead written in his own hand.

THE MACDONALD MASSACRE

SCOTLAND, 1692

The Scots have long been deeply divided over certain aspects of their history – clan chiefs often betrayed and even massacred each other's men at various times. In the nineteenth century a Scottish aristocracy that still does its best to ape the English aristocracy cleared tens of thousands of crofters from the land and replaced them with sheep.

Earlier betrayals are also legion – among the most famous was the massacre of the Macdonalds at Glencoe on 13 February 1692. Many myths and legends sprang up about this particularly brutal day, but among those well attested, though admittedly told in a number of slight variations, concerns the woman from Inverrigan and her baby. She escaped the massacre and hid with her child under a bridge over the Allt-na-Muidhe burn.

Unfortunately she could not prevent her child crying and a soldier was sent to kill it. The soldier found the woman but couldn't bring himself to kill her child so he stabbed the woman's dog instead and returned to his commander.

According to the story the officer insisted that the blood on the sword was not human blood and he told the soldier to return and kill the child, or be executed himself. The soldier returned to the woman and cut off one of the child's fingers to prove to the commanding officer that what he had ordered had been done.

Two decades later the soldier had long left the army and found himself crossing the moors late one night. He stopped at a remote cottage and asked if he could spend the night there. Then he sat for a long time by the fire describing his days soldiering and he told his host the most terrible thing he'd ever had to do – the tale of the woman at the bridge of Allt-na-Muidhe.

Before the old soldier left in the morning his host held up his hand and showed him a hand with the little finger missing.

BENBOW'S ANTICS

JAMAICA, 1702

The great, if slightly potty, Admiral Benbow died in Kingston, Jamaica in 1702. From his memorial tablet in St Mary's Church, Shrewsbury we discover that he was:

A skilful and daring seaman whose heroic exploits long rendered him the boast of the British Navy.

And still point him out as the Nelson of his times. He was born at Coton Hill in this Parish and died at Kingston in Jamaica November 4th 1702, aged 51 years of wounds received during his memorable action. With a French Squadron off Carthagena in the West Indies. Fought on the 19th and five following days of August in that year.

But that hardly hints at the real oddity of Benbow's exploits. For example, he once had a squadron of six ships under his command that were all ships owned by their captains. This was quite common at the end of the seventeenth century and it had advantages: men who owned their ships made sure they were well looked after, but there were disadvantages, too. When Benbow decided to engage the enemy during the wars with the French, the danger to his fellow captains' property was more important to them than winning the fight so they ran or, more properly, sailed away!

Why Benbow even bothered to try to conduct military operations under the circumstances is now hard to understand. With his squadron of six ships things were bound always to be rather uncertain and his final action came when he caught up with a French fleet of nine ships. They were armed merchant vessels, not nearly as heavily gunned as the British ships, but Benbow's fellow captains refused once again to take part in any military action (despite this being the reason why they were there in the first place) and huge potential booty was once again missed.

Benbow himself was so fed up with all this shilly-shallying that he attacked alone on this occasion and in a running fight that lasted several days his ship was badly damaged and Benbow himself badly injured. He later died from his wounds.

The French admiral, gracious in victory, sent a letter to Benbow saying he – Benbow – would undoubtedly have won their battle but for the hopeless cowardice of his fellow captains. As they were independent the captains simply carried on after Benbow's death – there was no formal military system to punish them, although there was a later attempt to court martial two of the captains.

It was Benbow's disaster that convinced the authorities back in England that an organised Navy was essential – private volunteers were just too unreliable. And thus it was that the Royal Navy was born.

HANNAH SNELL

ENGLAND, 1745

In 1750 James Gray returned from service with the Navy in the Far East. Gray – who was known as Hearty Jemmy – was notorious for fighting, drinking and whoring, but within a few weeks of his return he was to be exposed as a complete fraud. For James Gray was not a man at all: he was a widow in his twenties called Hannah Snell.

Hannah admitted having shared a room and a bed with dozens of male comrades in arms without once being discovered. During her military career – which lasted for more than five years – she had been wounded several times and flogged for various misdemeanors. It seems hard to credit, but despite all this and more, her identity as a woman was never even cause for suspicion. It was only after she retired with a war pension that her secret was finally disclosed – and she was the one who chose to reveal it.

Hannah's years of deception paid off because she had a second career as a theatrical performer – she danced and sang for many years at London's Sadler's Wells theatre where she was the star attraction dressed in full military regalia.

But her story starts in Worcester, where she was born in 1723. By the age of twenty-three she was married to a Dutch seaman. It was a big mistake and within a year he had deserted her.

Hannah was not one to take desertion lying down: she wanted to catch up with her errant husband and decided that the best way to do this was to join the Navy herself. She borrowed her cousin's clothes and his name, and in 1745 enlisted in Guise's Regiment of Foot.

She was signed on without question simply because, at that time, no one would have dreamed that a woman would even consider joining the Army. Within months, and following a flogging for insubordination, Hannah deserted the army and joined the Navy instead. She signed up at Portsmouth on the south coast. Clearly a bit of a rebel, she was quickly in trouble and flogged again, but this time she stayed at sea and by all accounts proved a doubty fighter in the Far Eastern wars. She was involved in hand-to-hand fighting just outside Madras in India, she dug trenches and latrines, waded through rivers and was wounded more than a dozen times.

Some time later, no one is sure exactly when, Hannah sailed for Lisbon, where she heard news that her husband had been executed. She refused to leave the Navy until her five years were up and she could claim her pension, which is exactly what she did. When she finally returned to London with her money she had her story printed and became the talk of the town. The Duke of Cumberland was so impressed that he put her name on the King's List to receive £30 a year for her wounds at Pondicherry.

She married again and opened a pub in Wapping called 'The Female Warrior', but for reasons that have never been explained she ended her days in the Bethlehem Hospital for the Insane. She died there in 1792.

INFANT SOLDIER

SRI LANKA, 1759

Tom Maitland, who was born in 1759, joined the army when he was just four days old – bizarre testament to the extraordinary system of buying commissions in the army in eighteenth century England. He did little fighting, it is true, till he was nineteen but then fought in an extraordinary series of campaigns across India and Ceylon, the West Indies and North America.

Maitland's career wasn't entirely glorious, however, and he behaved in ways that his contemporaries found absolutely extraordinary – for example, in 1798 he surrendered the town of Port Au Prince in Haiti in order to negotiate with the local black leader Toussaint l'Ouverture. At a time when most of the West viewed all black people as slaves and savages this was seen as an extraordinary decision.

But Maitland behaved in an entirely unconventional way: if he didn't like an order from his superiors he simply told them he had no intention of obeying them and that his idea was much better. Strangely, he was almost invariably proved right, which may explain why he was never cashiered or court martialled.

In 1805 he arrived in Ceylon, then a disorganised, highly corrupt state where the rule of law simply didn't exist, largely because the country was in a state of almost permanent civil war. Within months Maitland had turned Ceylon into one of the best-run countries in the Empire. He also compiled a series of books detailing every aspect of official life in Ceylon, from accounts and book keeping to rules for civil service payments. At the end of it Ceylon was well run and Maitland had saved the government more than £300,000 – tens of millions in today's values.

It wouldn't be fair to say that Maitland was often on the side of the native people, who were subject to the rule of the British Empire. But it often looked that way – when he was sent to help put down a mutiny in India he accused the local military commander Lord William Bentick of causing all the trouble in the first place by taking no account of local cultural sensitivities. Bentick had refused to allow native soldiers to wear traditional signs of the caste to which they belonged, for example.

Maitland also accused the British authorities in India of being too concerned with paperwork and doing things by the book at the expense of actually getting things done. In Ceylon he said that by contrast, 'there is nothing to be seen but results'.

Despite his maverick status he succeeded by results – he was eventually made Governor of Malta and then High Commissioner of the Ionian Islands. In Malta Maitland took charge immediately when an outbreak of disease threatened to engulf the island. He introduced strict quarantine restrictions and dozens of disinfectant and hygiene measures. All this was viewed as decidedly eccentric in an age when hygiene was thought to be of no significance but it was as nothing to the local people's astonished reaction to Maitland's appearance. The governor was normally dressed in the robes of his office and rarely, if ever, descended from his carriage. By contrast, Maitland seemed always to be walking across the island and dressed like a well-off tramp!

At official receptions he would often turn up in a dishevelled state, his shirt and breeks covered in snuff which he took continually along with strong drink. But even in the midst of his worst hangovers he would work long hours, dictating letters in an attempt to improve conditions on the island. At his funeral in 1824 the mourners were instructed to drink until they could drink no more – which they happily did.

HATLESS

GERMANY, 1760

The Blues are the only British regiment that allows saluting by all ranks even when the soldiers doing the saluting are not wearing any headdress. This bizarre tradition began after a brilliant charge by the regiment's colonel, the Marquis of Granby.

At the Battle of Warburg (during the Seven Years War) on 31 July 1760 Granby led his regiment in a charge against the French. So ferocious was the charge that Granby, in the thick of it, lost his hat and his wig. Despite this, and surrounded by a hail of musket balls and general chaos, he still managed to salute his commander in chief as he thundered by.

Granby was an unusually benevolent man – most discharged soldiers, even when badly disabled, were expected to fend for themselves or starve. Knowing how difficult this was, Granby set up many of his former soldier colleagues as innkeepers and this may explain the large number of British pubs called 'The Marquis of Granby'.

CATALOGUE OF CONFUSIONS

PRUSSIA, 1770

Frederick the Great (1740–86) took a personal interest in his armed forces, but particularly in his new young officers. He made it a habit to ask every new officer three questions. The first was: 'How old are you?' The second: 'How long have you been in my service?' And the third: 'Are you satisfied with your pay and treatment?'

One day Frederick was making his way among the latest batch of recruits when he reached a young Frenchman who, for reasons best known to himself, had decided to enlist in the Prussian army. The Frenchman didn't know a word of German, but his commanding officer, knowing that Frederick would want to talk to the new recruit, taught him the three answers he needed in order to respond to Frederick's three questions.

On the appointed day the new recruits assembled on the parade ground and Frederick made his way along, asking each man the usual three questions, but for reasons which no one ever discovered when the King came to the French recruit he decided to ask the second question first.

He asked: 'How long have you been in my service?' The young recruit, who'd been trained to respond by rote, thought that this must be the first question and replied: 'Twenty-one years.' The King was astonished, the soldier being clearly far too young to have served for that long. He then asked: 'How old are you?' 'One year' was the inevitable answer. Even more astonished, the King said: 'Well, one of us has taken leave of our senses.'

Thinking this was the third question, the soldier said: 'Both, if it please your worship.' 'This is the first time in my life that I have been treated as if I were a madman!' said the King. He then tried to ask a few more questions to see if he could find out why the young man was so perplexing. Immediately the young man responded in French that he did not understand a word of German and the mystery was solved. The King roared with laughter, patted the young soldier on the back and left.

A COMPANY OF IDIOTS

AMERICA, 1775

If the British really wanted to keep its American colonies, you would never have guessed it from the bizarre decisions they took now and then about how to keep the huge new continent.

In many British military campaigns in America the first concern of King George's government seemed to be to alienate the colonists; worse, when they decided it was time to put down any sort of insurrection they often sent the least trained and most ill-fitted troops to do their work.

A good example of this bizarre behaviour occurred in 1775. At this time the British were still fighting the French for possession of various parts of the Americas and the French, who had been causing trouble along the Ohio River, had built a stronghold at Fort Dequesne. The British decided to show the French and their Indian allies who was boss. But in a way that was to become typical of virtually all British military adventures in America the British government underestimated the abilities of both the French and the Indians, just as later on they were to underestimate the abilities of the colonists themselves during the War of Independence.

The Fort Dequesne strategy, thought up by British military intelligence, was to send what were generally acknowledged to be the two worst regiments in the British army – Sir Peter Hackett's 48th Foot and Colonel Tom Dunbar's 44th Foot. Both regiments were said to be full of disaffected trouble-makers; they were ill disciplined and disliked both their superiors and each other. Yet the British government decided that they would be just the men to beat the French in America.

The soldiers' contempt for their leaders was matched by their contempt for the man who was eventually chosen to take overall command. Major General Edward Braddock was fat and slow, and in more than forty years of military service he had neither seen nor heard a shot fired in anger. What made him even worse was that he was utterly convinced of his own abilities and of the uselessness of his adversary. He simply assumed that as an English gentleman he would be able to win: both against the French and against the Indians.

Braddock insisted that the main tactic would be to use the standard British army manoeuvre known as wheel and fire. This worked well enough in the sort of open field battles typical of European warfare, but it was worse than useless in the dense forest through which his men were now marching. Against the Indian's guerilla tactics wheel and fire was hopeless, yet each time his men were attacked Braddock ordered the wheel and fire tactic to be used.

Even before they began to come under attack Braddock's army was in trouble: their food went bad, their horses wandered off and the men started to desert. They'd landed at Alexandria and had almost one hundred miles to travel to reach Fort Duquesne. Their guides were Indians in the pay of the British but long before they reached the French fort, most of these guides had deserted simply because they were so badly treated by Braddock. As they came closer to the fort the soldiers began to be picked off by the Indians. Their scalps were left nailed to trees as a grisly reminder of the fate that lay in store for their fellows.

A dozen or so miles before they reached the fort the British were attacked by the French and their Indian allies, who had come out to meet them – weakened by hunger, desertions and appalling leadership the British were virtually annihilated. In the intense heat they still wore heavy red uniforms and were commanded to try to fight using the wheel and fire manoeuvre. But it was the prospect of being scalped that really won the day for the French. At first sight of the French troops' Indian allies the British soldiers were so terrified they ran. Braddock and his fellow officers were killed (Braddock was helped away, but died later) and the battle remains as one of the most bizarre and stupid British military blunders in the Americas.

HOPPING MAD

AMERICA, 1779

During the siege of the British garrison at Savannah during the American War of Independence, Samuel Warren fought on the side of the rebels. Some years earlier he'd defected from the British Army and was absolutely devoted to the cause of independence. But members of his family were outraged at his perceived disloyalty. So much so, in fact, that on hearing that he was involved in the siege, his aunt wrote to him to say that she hoped – if it was true and he really was fighting with the rebels – that he would lose a leg.

A few days after receiving his aunt's letter Warren was hit by a cannon ball, which cleanly removed one of his legs. He survived the ordeal and had the bone from his lost leg cleaned and preserved. When the war was over he ordered a mahogany case from a local cabinet maker and had the leg carefully mounted in it. He then sent the display case to his aunt with a note to say that, while her wish had come true, he would still rather be a rebel with one leg than a royalist with two!

BLUE NOSE

ENGLAND, 1794

That great king of fashion, Beau Brummel, was an officer in the 10th Light Dragoons. Commissioned by his friend the Prince Regent he was forgiven for being not quite the most brilliant military man, but even the prince could not always save him from embarrassment, for Brummel was one of England's most forgetful soldiers.

His biggest difficulty was that he could never remember the faces of the men in the troop he commanded – it was a chronic problem that led to huge embarrassment and there seemed to be no solution. But then as now, incompetence was no bar to high rank in the British army provided one had the right accent and background, which, of course, Brummel had.

Brummel himself came up with a solution – he noticed that one of the men in his troop had a very blue nose and he ordered that this man should always be in the front rank when the men were assembled. If Brummel then failed to identify his troop of men he would need only to look for that blue nose to know that he was in the right place.

All went well until one day Brummel sat immaculately dressed on his splendid horse and was approached by a senior officer, who demanded what he thought he was doing. Brummel stared in blank amazement at the squadron commander. 'You are with the wrong troop,' he was told in no uncertain terms. Panic stricken, Brummel stared around and with a sigh of relief spotted the blue nose in the men lined up just in front of him. 'I think, if I may say so, you are mistaken,'

44

he replied. 'I'm not so foolish as to be unable to recognise my own troop.' But what Brummel, who famously spent most of his army career in front of a mirror, did not know was that there had been a reorganisation and, without his knowledge, Blue Nose had been moved to another troop.

RABBIT MAN

FRANCE, 1800

While his star was in the ascendant everyone in France treated Napoleon as a god, but this led to absurd levels of deference with his fellow soldiers and ministers falling over themselves to organise things in such a way that the Emperor always had the best of everything. Sometimes this led to wonderfully absurd disasters.

When Napoleon expressed a desire to go shooting, for example, the army commander Berthier did his utmost to make sure that the day went with military precision. Every detail was worked out in advance and, leaving nothing to chance, Berthier bought more than a thousand rabbits and had them released in the grounds of the Tuileries where the shoot was due to take place. On the morning of the shoot, the Emperor's carriage rolled into the gardens followed by the carriages of his favourites and flunkies.

The Emperor was so convinced of his own greatness that he may well have decided the game would throw itself in front of him, only too pleased to be shot by such a great man. He took his gun and walked ahead of the others into the park, ready it seemed for action.

Berthier looked on, knowing that soon the Emperor would come across masses of game in the form of the one thousand odd rabbits he had earlier released. What the army commander did not know, however, was that he had bought tame rabbits, not wild ones – and these rabbits were used to being fed regularly by a man who walked out towards them twice a day.

So when Napoleon advanced, gun in hand, the rabbits all thought this was the man who came each day to feed them. Rather than run away, they ran towards him. History does not record what Napoleon thought when all one thousand rabbits appeared at the same time and rushed at him. Mortified, Berthier and the other courtiers tried to beat off the rabbits using sticks and whips, but the bunnies were too quick for them and whirled and wheeled about, returning again and again to the feet of the man who should have brought their lunch.

MARSHAL STOCKPOT

FRANCE, 1801

During the Napoleonic wars a French sergeant decided that the war was no fun at all and that he would be far better off relaxing and enjoying himself well behind the lines. He explained his plan to more than a hundred of his fellow soldiers, who decided to join him. The merry band set off for a large deserted convent some miles back from the front and here they set up home.

The best thing about the convent was that it was still well provided with stores of food, comfortable beds and other furniture. Marshal Stockpot, as the leader of this merry gang became known, sent his soldiers out into the surrounding countryside each day to find whatever they could in the way of food. Soon the men were living like kings with food constantly being cooked in vast stew pots and masses of wine and brandy available to all at any time of the day or night.

Soon the convent attracted a number of women and the nights of debauchery became legendary. Months passed and the numbers swelled to about three hundred. Then, as with all good things, Marshal Stockpot's convent came unstuck. A band of soldiers who really were still soldiers were foraging near the convent and discovered a small flock of sheep. They were in the process of driving the sheep off when Marshal Stockpot appeared and told them that they could not have them.

But the soldiers refused to hand the sheep back and Marshal Stockpot and his men immediately attacked – his French followers refused to fire, but a number of English and Portuguese ex-soldiers who were with him did fire and several

French soldiers were killed and injured. The foraging party set off back to their commanding officers. Accompanying them were the French soldiers, who had formerly deserted but now decided that shooting their former colleagues was a step too far.

The French deserters who returned to their units were told they would be given a pardon if they took a much larger contingent of men and attacked Marshal Stockpot, and this they did. The next day Stockpot, along with his English and Portuguese followers, was captured and shot.

FEMME FATALE

SPAIN, 1812

One of the most extraordinary stories from any military campaign in history concerns the appearance of a young woman called Juanita during the fierce fighting at Badajoz in Spain. She was eventually to give her name to the town of Ladysmith in South Africa but her first appearance was perhaps the most remarkable incident in her life.

Juanita simply appeared one day among the officers' tents of the British army. As soon as an officer approached her, she explained that she was a member of an ancient Spanish family and that her husband was an officer in the Spanish army, but she feared he was dead. She was with her sister and she explained that they were now homeless.

She so impressed the English officers that within days she had met and agreed to marry Harry Smith of the Rifle Brigade – and she was to spend the next forty years with him, dying eventually in South Africa.

BROLLIES

FRANCE, 1813

During heavy fighting near Bayonne in 1813 the Grenadier Guards found themselves hanging around for days on end in an almost continual downpour. So fed up did they become that the officers equipped themselves with umbrellas and simply sat in their redoubt with these umbrellas up, looking for all the world, according to one commentator, as if they were loitering in Piccadilly Circus.

The guards were under the command of Colonel Tynling, who saw nothing wrong with the umbrellas, given the nature of the downpour – virtually a deluge – and the fact that his regiment was not yet in action. However, Wellington happened to pass by, saw the huge number of open umbrellas and was not pleased. 'Lord Wellington does not approve of the use of umbrellas during the enemy's firing,' he said, 'they will make us look ridiculous in the eyes of the enemy.'

Colonel Tynling was reprimanded by Lord Wellington, who concluded: 'The guards may in uniform when on duty at St James's carry umbrellas if they please, but in the field it is not only ridiculous but unmilitary.'

A VALUABLE DONKEY

BELGIUM, 1814

Of all Wellington's soldiers Henry Francis Mellish was one of the most eccentric. A captain in the 10th Hussars he was constantly getting into scrapes but somehow, as Wellington himself acknowledged, he always got out of them.

But on the day Mellish was captured by the French it was assumed that he would not be seen again or at least not for some considerable time. When Wellington heard that he had been taken prisoner, he merely remarked that the French 'would not keep him long'. As usual in such matters, Wellington was proved right.

A few days after his disappearance Mellish was spotted heading towards the British lines – bizarrely he was riding a donkey. This caused much hilarity among Mellish's fellow officers because it would have been far better if he had lost his horse or had it shot from under him. In such circumstances, £35 in government compensation was always paid. Mellish was unperturbed. Having rested, he took off again on his donkey toward the French lines and said, 'I'll soon make my £35.' He then rode till he was well within range of the French gunners, had the poor old donkey shot from under him and returned to claim his £35.

ADDICTED TO WAR

INDIA, 1814

Every so often the military produces an individual so addicted to fighting that he'd really rather be dead than give it up. One such character was Rollo Gillespie, an Irishman who joined the 3rd Irish Horse Regiment straight from school and spent the rest of his life fighting in various hotspots round the globe.

Gillespie's military career began with a duel in Ireland for which he was due to be prosecuted when he escaped to Scotland before returning to stand trial. He was acquitted on the grounds of justifiable homicide in 1788. Obsessed with the army and the military life he immediately joined the Jamaica Light Dragoons and was sent overseas. His ship foundered off the coast of Madeira and Gillespie spent weeks on the brink of death after contracting yellow fever. When he recovered, he set sail again for the West Indies, where the British were locked in a bitter conflict with the French.

He fought at Port-au-Prince and at several other major battles. Then, while at St. Domingo, he was asleep one night when a band of robbers broke into his house. There were eight of them but Gillespie cared nothing about death and injury, and this may be the reason he managed to kill six of them before the other two fled.

Back in England by 1805 he set off across Europe, through Greece and Iraq until he reached India. He could have led a quiet life now but was, as he once admitted, addicted to the profession of arms. So he set off in pursuit of glory once again and in 1806 he helped put down a mutiny at Vellore, where he was famously hauled up to the battlements in a basket to take command.

By 1812 Gillespie had moved on to Sumatra, where he deposed the Sultan. Back in India he was at the races when a tiger strayed on to the course. He immediately ran out and killed the animal with a single shot. By 1814 he was attacking a Nepalese hill fort with a party of the 8th Dragoons. Attack after attack failed, but Gillespie – once described as the most single-minded man in the British army – refused to give up and it was on the third or fourth attempt to take the fort that he was shot through the heart.

LEGLESS

BELGIUM, 1815

The English reputation for suffering untold pain and indignity with the proverbial stiff upper lip has an important basis in truth. Whatever one thinks of the jingoism and racial attitudes of earlier generations there was a tradition of stoicism that was unique to the British establishment, but particularly that part of the establishment that produced generation after generation of sons whose only wish was to follow their fathers into the services. At its best this produced men of the utmost loyalty and diligence; at worst men of unfeeling brutality. It also produced legendary figures whose bravery is astonishing by any standards, regardless of whatever one might now think of the cause in which that bravery revealed itself.

One of the finest examples occurred at the Battle of Waterloo, where Lord Uxbridge was injured. Writing decades after the event Uxbridge himself recalled that he was hit: 'in the low ground beyond Le Haye Sainte and perhaps a quarter of an hour before dusk at the moment when I was quitting the duke to join the brigade of Hussars which I had sent for, being the only fresh corps I had'.

Others remembered a far less dispassionate account. One soldier who was nearby recalled Lord Uxbridge, then riding close to Wellington, suddenly shout: 'By God, Sir, I've lost my leg!' Wellington took his telescope away from his eye, glanced at Uxbridge and said mildly, 'So you have,' and then returned to his watch of the battlefield.

But whatever Uxbridge or Wellington's reaction at that

55

moment, we know that a large ball hit and shattered Uxbridge's knee and left the leg horribly mangled and bleeding profusely. Back at the field hospital the surgeons examined the leg and announced that if it didn't come off immediately Uxbridge would quickly die. Legend has it that Uxbridge said: 'Well gentlemen, I thought as much myself. I have put myself in your hands and if it is to be taken off, the sooner it is done the better.'

The surgeons then prepared their saws and knives, and Uxbridge watched with apparent equanimity. He chatted to his aides about the course of the battle, the great victory they had achieved and the irony of his having been hit by one of the last shots in the last part of the battle. Some even said he was hit by the very last shot of all.

An officer who was there when the amputation took place later wrote:

He never moved or complained. No one even held his hand. He only said once that he thought the instrument was not sharp. When it was over his nerves did not seem the least shaken and the surgeons said his pulse was not altered. He said, smiling: 'I have had a pretty long run. I have been a beau these forty-seven years and it would not be fair to cut the young men out longer.' I have seen many operations but neither Lord Greenock nor myself could bear this, we were obliged to go to the other end of the room.

A friend of Uxbridge's, who came to see him in his tent that night, reported that he seemed untroubled and merely said, 'Take a look at that leg, would you, and tell me what you think of it. Some time hence perhaps I may be inclined to imagine it might have been saved and I should like your opinion.' His visitor looked at the severed leg, which was lying nearby, and confirmed that it was much better off.

A small coffin was made a few days later and the leg solemnly buried with an inscription explaining to whom it belonged and how it had came to be buried. Beneath this official inscription someone later wrote:

    Here lies the Marquis of Anglesey's Limb
    The Devil will have the remainder of him.

Many years later Uxbridge, by then an old man, returned to the house where his leg had been removed and found the table on which the operation had been performed. He insisted that he and his guests should eat their dinner that evening round the table – which they did.

WATERLOO ESCAPES

BELGIUM, 1815

It's easy to forget how different battles were before mechanisation, tanks, motor vehicles, airplanes and heavy guns. Ball and musket shot was deadly, but its full force could be deflected in a way that simply wouldn't happen with a modern, high-powered round.

This is probably why in so many early conflicts there are amazing tales of escape from what must have seemed like certain death or injury – amazing, because they relied on fluke events and million-to-one chances. The Battle of Waterloo seems to have had far more than its fair share of extraordinary escapes. Take the case of Sir George Scovell who, standing amid the thick of the fighting, raised his arm to stop his hat blowing off. He then looked down to see that the armpit of his jacket had been shot away – if he hadn't lifted his arm at that precise moment his whole shoulder would have been smashed by the shot and he'd have bled quickly to death.

Sergeant John Flesh of the 16th Light Dragoons is another good example. Flesh was hit full on in the chest and knocked flat on his back by a musket ball. He was badly knocked about and so winded that he thought he would die – until someone noticed the musket ball rolling out of his uniform. The shot had clearly hit something else before it hit Sergeant Flesh and most of its energy was spent – it had enough force to get through the thick material of his jacket, but left little more than a bruise on his skin. Even more amazing is that a few moments later as he recovered himself he was hit again by another shot that had ricocheted from the body of a dead soldier lying nearby. Again, he was completely unharmed.

Finally, there is the extraordinary case of Lieutenant Edward Peters of the 7th Hussars. He was hit full in the chest by a small cannon ball – he was knocked to the ground and remained unconscious for some time – but when examined, he was found to be completely uninjured. The cannon ball crashed into his raised sword using up most of his energy in the process before hitting the soldier in the chest.

WATERLOO TEETH

BELGIUM, 1815

For centuries, right up until the modern era – and in some conflicts into it – one of the great attractions of warfare for the ordinary soldier was the chance of looting. This might mean looting shops and houses overrun during a battle, or more likely the chance to rob the enemy dead, assuming the looters were not themselves killed.

At Waterloo such was the scale of loss of life that there were very rich pickings indeed for the British troops when the battle was over. Soldiers were reputedly burdened down with watches, lockets, swords and pistols. Those taken from dead officers were often of the finest make or encrusted with jewels and gold, and many ordinary soldiers collected enough booty in the afternoon after the great battle to live comfortably for the rest of their lives back in England.

When the watches and purses had been taken there were the gold epaulettes, gold braid, the fine clothes and equipment. And once the dead had been stripped, their teeth were taken for, in that era, real human teeth from the dead – or from the poor who sold theirs while they were still alive – were used to make false teeth. At Waterloo such a vast number of teeth were taken from the dead that for many years afterwards and indeed, well into the middle decades of the nineteenth century, dentures in England were known as 'Waterloo teeth'.

THE CONGREVE ROCKET

Sir William Congreve (1772–1828) came from a long line of military inventors. His father was superintendent of the Royal Military Repository at Woolwich and controller of the Royal Laboratory. Sir William was asked to look into the possibility of producing military rockets and by 1809 he'd come up with a bizarre, but apparently workable system.

The first Congreve Rocket involved the explosive head being attached to the side of the rocket shaft. This badly affected the balance and, when fired, the rocket was as likely to turn round and kill the person who'd fired it as it was the enemy.

By 1815 Congreve realised this was a major flaw and the rocket was re-designed to allow the explosive head to be mounted on the end of the shaft with the shaft attached at the mid-point of the base of the head. This made for far greater accuracy, but it was still very primitive and eccentric to say the least – soldiers were terrified to use it; Wellington detested it. One of his captains, Captain Mercer, left a first-hand description of the Congreve Rocket in action: 'Our rocketeers kept shooting off rockets, none of which ever followed the course of the first. Most of them, on arriving about the middle of the ascent, took a vertical direction, whilst some actually turned back upon ourselves, and one of these, following me like a squib until its shell exploded, actually put me in more danger than all the fire of the enemy throughout the day'.

At Waterloo more than fifty rockets were fired but there is no record of them inflicting a single casualty on the French though they may well have knocked out a few British troops! Another commentator who saw them in action said: 'The rockets did not seem to answer very well. They certainly made a most tremendous noise, and were formidable spitfires – no cavalry could stand if they came near them, but there seemed the difficulty. None went within half a mile of the intended object and the direction seemed excessively uncertain. The ground was very bad, and on a flat, or along a road, where they would ricochet or bound along straight they might do very well, but in our case they went bang into the ground; some pieces of the shell came back even amongst us spectators'.

AFTER THE WAR WAS OVER

AMERICA, 1815

The Battle of New Orleans took place in January 1815 even though the war of which it was part had ended two weeks earlier. The reason for this bizarre situation was that communications were so bad that news of the end of the war took almost three weeks to reach Louisiana!

But the battle was still officially part of the Anglo American war of 1812–14. On the British side Sir Edward Packenham (1778–1815), brother-in-law of the Duke of Wellington, led an expeditionary force whose aim was the capture of New Orleans. That strategic victory would have prevented the Americans gaining access to the Mississippi River. The British stopped and began their battle planning on the banks of the great river, but it was never going to be easy. Up ahead the American leader Major General Andrew Jackson had the river to his right and an impenetrable swamp on the left; in front he had a clear line of fire to any approaching enemy. Across this front, hidden behind an earth rampart, he'd positioned over four thousand riflemen. He'd also used a series of massively built brick kilns as forward posts; his frontline soldiers were supported by artillery batteries to the rear. Out on the river the warship USS Louisiana was ready to support the land troops with eighteen heavy cannon. On the opposite river bank General Morgan waited with more than a thousand soldiers and yet more heavy guns.

Edward Pakenham must have been awed by the force opposing him but he was extremely well supplied with men –

some seven thousand in all – including a flanking brigade ready to cross the river and fight Morgan's troops in an attempt to outflank the Americans.

The British attack began at night so that Packenham's troops would have a chance to cross the river undetected. Things were complicated by the fact that elaborate earthworks had already been built to keep the British flotilla of boats from being swept away by the strong waters of the Mississippi. On the night of the crossing the earthworks failed and caused a serious delay to the British troops' attempts to cross the river.

When the rocket went up and the land battle began in the morning, Pakenham's right wing was immediately thrown into confusion by poor discipline and organisation; the Americans were also directing their fire with deadly effect. That said, the British eventually reached and secured part of the Americans' earthwork defences. On the left flank the advance was better – in fact several American positions were taken before Colonel Robert Rennie was killed and the momentum went out of the British attack. As the light improved, three more commanding officers on the British side were killed. Sustaining heavy losses, the British finally fell back.

On the West Bank, meanwhile, the British forces led by Colonel Thornton somehow realised with great insight that the American position was lightly defended. Thornton charged with the minimum of preparation – he succeeded in pushing the Americans back and was hugely successful – but his efforts were all in vain as the main British attack on the other side of the river had completely failed.

British losses were huge: nearly three hundred were killed and more than a thousand badly injured. Just thirteen Americans were killed and forty wounded – and, of course, it was pointless anyway as the war was already over.

WOMAN WITH A PAST

ENGLAND, 1821

Phoebe Hessel was reputed to be 107 when she died in Brighton, Sussex, in 1821, but even more remarkable is the fact that as a young woman she is said to have fought in the British Army for some seventeen years.

Born in Stepney, East London in 1713, Phoebe married Samuel Golding, a soldier, and decided that if he had to go to war then she'd rather go with him than be parted. She later claimed they'd fought together in the 5th regiment of foot under the Duke of Cumberland in America and the West Indies. Fighting in disguise she was wounded several times, receiving a serious bayonet wound in the arm on one occasion.

After the Battle of Fontenoy in 1745 Phoebe confessed her secret to the Colonel's wife and was honourably discharged, along with her husband who received a pension. When Golding died – and his pension with him – Phoebe married a Mr Hessel and when he in turn died (Phoebe seems to have outlived almost everyone!), she became an itinerant fish seller wandering the lanes and villages around Brighton. She also made a little money by trading on her fame – visitors to the hugely popular Regency town sought her out to hear her tales and see her war wound. When life as a travelling saleswoman became too much Phoebe took to selling toys and other trinkets, as well as gingerbread and apples from a stall on the corner of Marine Parade.

By 1808 her fame had brought her to the attention of the Prince Regent and she was awarded an annual pension. In the last year of her life, when the Prince Regent became King George IV in 1821, she was carried in a horse and carriage to the Coronation celebrations. So smitten was George IV that he arranged for Phoebe to be given a fine burial in St. Nicholas' Churchyard in Brighton, where her gravestone can still be seen.

SUBMERSIBLE

AMERICA, 1836

Submarines seem so modern that it is difficult to believe they have a long history, but at least as far back as the eighteenth century attempts were made to build an airtight vessel that could at least be lowered safely beneath the waves. Although metalworking wasn't really up to the task at the time, the basic ideas being deployed by those early marine engineers were pretty sound.

By the mid-nineteenth century the rapid technological developments of the ongoing industrial revolution meant a submarine that could go under water and also manoeuvre itself independently of any mother ship on the surface was a real possibility. One of the earliest, and maddest, of these submarines was a pedal powered shallow water submersible invented in the 1830s for the American militia by Mr Lodner D. Phillips from Indiana. Cigar shaped, with a glass bubble rising midway along the main body, the Phillips' submarine was entirely powered by pedals. In fact, the internal arrangement was rather like a recumbent cycle. The submariner (there was room only for one) sat in the middle of the submarine with his head in the glass bubble and the pedals operated a small propeller at the back through a complex series of chains, cogs and rods.

In clear water with no obstructions the Phillips submarine was capable of a few knots an hour. Its buoyancy tanks were incredibly inefficient, however – it was constantly becoming up-ended or nose-diving! With no lights or radar, it quickly foundered in murky water, but it was a step in the right direction.

Phillips, who incidentally was a shoemaker by profession, built a second submarine that was hand-cranked along at speeds up to four knots. It could also dive to depths of about a hundred feet but again, without lights and navigation equipment it never had a clue where it was and constantly crashed into underwater obstacles. Nothing daunted, Mr Phillips offered to sell the patent for his idea to the United States military but they dismissed the submarine as an idea with no future and explained that the United States Navy was in the business of floating on, rather than under, the sea.

UNIFYING

ITALY, 1848

Giusseppe Garibaldi (1807–1882) must be one of the oddest, yet most successful, military leaders in modern history. Despite his complete lack of formal education – he was virtually illiterate – he managed to defeat the Catholic Church and the Papacy, as well as King Victor Emmanuel of Piedmont to achieve his vision of a united Italy. At the beginning of Garibaldi's career this was a prospect that seemed like a mad impossible dream.

Born in 1807 in Nice, which was then held by Italy, as a young man Garibaldi went to South America before returning to Italy in what became known across Europe as the Year of Revolution: 1848. During the Italian contribution to the revolution the Pope's hated first minister Rossi was assassinated. The Pope himself was then driven out of Rome by a popular rising and the reaction of the French was to invade Italy to support the Pope.

Garibaldi was already leading a band of Revolutionaries. Hopelessly outnumbered, he attacked the regular French Army and against all the odds he defeated them. He was a brilliant guerilla fighter, who frequently succeeded against all the odds, but even he suffered an occasional setback. One of the worst came in 1849 during an attack on the Villa Corsini. Many of Garibaldi's men were killed in this action but, rather than give up he and his remaining men simply led a tenacious and continuing guerilla war against the French, Spanish and Austrian forces that now occupied Rome.

Garibaldi caused the military huge problems but regular betrayals of his men – usually by priests – meant that in 1850 he had to leave Italy for America. A few years later he returned and became a farmer, living quietly, well away from politics. Then out of the blue the Prime Minister of Piedmont, Camillo Benso di Cavour, called him back from obscurity to lead the Piedmontese Army.

In 1859 Garibaldi defeated the Austrians at Castaletto on Lake Maggiore; he then went to Southern Italy to encourage a popular rising. He defeated a Neapolitan Army but was wounded in 1861 during a battle at Aspromonte. Though captured, he was soon released and found time to visit England, where he was lionised.

By 1865 he was back in a largely united Italy – the only exceptions were Venice and Rome. In 1870, with the defeat of France by Bismarck, French troops withdrew but it wasn't finally until the World War One that the last few Italian cities joined a united nation. Even today Rome is a separate state within a state.

What makes Garibadli so extraordinary is that he achieved with military resources a success that seemed to almost everyone else a complete impossibility.

ON THE MARCH

AFGHANISTAN, 1842

Florentia Wynch was a young woman who'd led a sheltered life until, in her early twenties, she married Captain Robert Sale. The captain saw service in one of Britain's least successful Victorian military campaigns – in Afghanistan – and his wife went with him. Lady Sale, as she had become, also took part in the extraordinary march from Kabul, in which all but a handful of the fourteen thousand who took part in the march died. She was later imprisoned by the Afghans.

At the time of the march Lady Sale was 54. She'd given birth to twelve children and was not in the best of health. Yet during the long foot-slogging journey she tended the sick and wounded, the women and children. She was twice wounded herself but despite hunger and danger she managed to write a detailed diary, which is now considered one of the most remarkable documents from the first Afghan War (1838–42) – a war that led eventually to the complete withdrawal of the British in 1880.

Lady Sale's diary is a calm, measured, detailed account of terrible privations – she witnessed brutal battles, massacres, earthquakes and hardship. On one occasion she offered to lead a reluctant group of soldiers into battle and, when badly injured by a bullet in the arm, she observed dryly: 'I had, fortunately, only one ball in my arm.'

Lady Sale was eventually released by her Afghan captors and she returned to England, where Queen Victoria was so impressed and astonished by her exploits that she awarded her an annual pension of £500. When Lady Sale died, aged sixty-six, her tombstone was carved with the following words: 'Under this stone reposes all that could die of Lady Sale'.

TERROR QUEEN

MADAGASCAR, 1840

One of the world's oddest and most ferocious military leaders was the splendidly named Queen Ranavalona I Rabodo-andrianampoinimerina (1828–61) of Madagascar. Known as Ranavalo-Manyka I, or Ranavalona I, in 1840 when almost a child she was married to King Radama but was later accused of having poisoned him at the request of protestant English missionaries who had befriended her.

The couple were childless, so English missionaries helped Ranavalona become Queen in her own right. Having been crowned Queen, she immediately had all her relatives assassinated. She expelled all foreigners and using her twenty-thousand-strong all-male army she crushed all opposition.

In 1829 the French Government secretly conspired to have the Queen deposed but she was far too shrewd and wily for this, and their attempt failed. Queen Ranavalona I largely took revenge on the few Europeans left on the island and made her lover Rainitaiarivoy (1828–96) Prime Minister despite the fact that he was hated across the island. She remains one of the world's few brutal – and female – military dictators.

WHISTLER IN THE DARK

AMERICA, 1853

It is a little known fact, but a fact none the less, that the celebrated painter James Whistler (1834–1903) was once a cadet in the United States Army and, despite his later fame, he was one of the worst army cadets in American history.

General Webb would later remember Whistler's disastrous showing at cavalry drill. More often than not he would slide over the horse's head each and every time it stopped, never seeming to improve despite the passage of time and his increasing experience. With delicious sarcasm Whistler's commanding officer, on watching the future painter fall for the umpteenth time over the front of the horse, would call out: 'Mr Whistler, aren't you a little ahead of the squad?'

On one occasion Whistler had flopped backward and forward several times before he finally fell heavily to the ground. A soldier ran to help him up and a nearby Major called out: 'Mr Whistler, are you hurt?' To which Whistler replied: 'No, Major, but I do not understand how any man can keep a horse for his own amusement!'

AN ASTONISHING VICTORY

The Battle of Balaclava was one of those seminal moments in British military history – a moment that helped convince the British that, when it came to valour, they really were a cut above the rest.

Sir Colin Campbell and his force were protecting Balaclava from attack during the Crimean War (1854–56). The Russian army was at last close enough to open fire with a real chance of inflicting serious casualties on Sir Colin's men and almost certainly breaking through to Balaclava itself. The difficulty was that Campbell's men were on a hillock at the entrance to a gorge that led to Balaclava but they were exposed. All they could do was lie on the open hillside and try to accept the bombardment that then began – an exceptionally nerve-wracking experience.

As the shells rained down around them Sir Colin noticed that the Russian cavalry was advancing toward them. The Turkish part of Sir Colin's army immediately took to their heels and fled back towards Balaclava. It was said that as they passed an encampment of the Argylls' a soldier's wife ran out and attacked them for cowardice, kicking and shouting at them as they passed.

There were now just five hundred and fifty men between the huge Russian army and Balaclava, and Sir Colin told his men they could, under no circumstances, retreat and they must defend their position or die in the attempt. But the fact that they were mostly lying down – because of the artillery shelling

75

and their relatively small number – Campbell's soldiers had an initial stroke of enormous luck. The mighty Russian cavalry bearing down on them almost certainly assumed the hillock was empty. When they were within rifle shot of the hillock they must have been astonished when two lines of Highland soldiers in bright red coats sprang to their feet and fired. The Russians were taken aback – what could this mean?

The line that was immortalised as the thin red line fired again and again, and before their eyes the might of the Russian cavalry twitched nervously and failed to advance further. More shots and the Highlanders – eager now to engage the enemy – moved forward. Unsure how many they faced, the Russians turned tail and fled back to their lines. Rarely has the British army's sense of its own brilliance enjoyed a greater boost.

SOMETHING'S COOKING

RUSSIA, 1855

Despite the resistance of army chiefs Florence Nightingale transformed the lives of soldiers fighting in the Crimean War and her efforts also meant that in future conflicts soldiers could no longer be treated worse than animals. From then on some kind of rudimentary decency was established in military and field hospitals. The idea that filthy conditions and inadequate food kept the men tough disappeared, which was no bad thing given that a huge percentage of the casualties at the Crimea before Florence Nightingale's arrival were actually caused by the appalling conditions in which the men had to live and not by anything inflicted by the enemy.

But what Florence Nightingale did for the men's health, the celebrated French chef Alexis Soyer did for their food in one of military history's most unusual turnarounds. Soyer was London's most famous chef – he made lunch at the Reform Club one of the major delights of living in London. But London society was astonished when at his own expense, having heard about the appalling food eaten by soldiers, he set off for Russia at the height of the war.

In appearance, according to one observer, he was like a comic opera Frenchman but, when Florence Nightingale met him, she knew at once that he was a man of enormous talent and commitment. Commenting on his abilities, she wrote: 'Others have studied cooking for the purpose of gour-mandising, some for show, but none for the purpose of cooking large quantities of food in the most nutritive and economical manner for great quantities of people'.

The military authorities, resistant as ever to change, were not welcoming but Soyer had the backing of some very powerful people, including Lord Panmure, and he insisted on changing everything. Virtually inedible army rations were used to make what were quickly agreed to be the most delicious soups and stews. He absolutely insisted that the army kitchen practice of boiling everything should be abolished and he stopped the practice of using any old soldier who happened to be available to man the stewpots. Instead he selected a group of soldiers who were to be based permanently in the kitchens and had the talent to be trained as cooks.

Before Soyer, bread could not be made for the soldiers. But he invented a new type of oven that not only made delicious bread but biscuits, too, and he invented a special teapot – thereafter known as the 'Scutari teapot' – that could keep enough tea hot at any one time for fifty men.

Whenever he appeared the men cheered him to the rafters, but one of his reforms was never accepted. Before Soyer, weight was the sole principle on which meat was divided up between the men but as the meat was never boned, it meant that many men were given only bone. Soyer insisted a fairer system would be to take out the bones and use them for soup while dividing up the meat only between the men. With typical bureaucratic idiocy, however, he was told this would not be possible because it would take a new service regulation to achieve it.

FIRST VC

FINLAND, 1854

It's often been said that in order to win the Victoria Cross you have to behave in a way so reckless that you are almost certain to lose your life – which is why so many VCs are awarded posthumously. The very first VC ever awarded is a good example of the risks you have to take and of the amazing bravery – or foolhardiness – involved.

During the Crimean War Charles Lucas was serving aboard HMS *Hecla* in the Baltic. It was 21 June 1854 and *Hecla* and two of her sister ships had been bombarding Bomarsund, a fort on an island off Finland. To the consternation of the ship's crew, their fire was suddenly returned with a vengeance. Before the men on deck could take cover a live shell landed right in the middle of the deck, but failed to explode. It rolled ominously, its fuse still hissing, and the men were immediately ordered to lie flat on the deck. Then, without a thought for his own safety – as the citation was later to put it – Charles Lucas ran forward and, with great presence of mind, picked up the red hot shell and hurled it into the sea. But it was a close run thing as the shell exploded in mid air. Thanks to Lucas's action the ship was unscathed and not a single injury sustained.

DISASTROUS CHARGE

RUSSIA, 1854

The charge of the Light Brigade at Balaclava has become a symbol for the glorious folly of bravery in the face of overwhelming odds and prefigures in miniature the slaughter that later came to symbolise the Great War (1914–18). But it is easy to forget – when we think of suicidal bravery – just how completely insane from a military point of view the charge really was. In fact, there is strong evidence that it was all an incompetent mistake.

The charge was ultimately the responsibility of Lord Raglan, who was famously eccentric. At Waterloo, forty years earlier, he lost an arm and after the surgeon had cut it off and walked away, Raglan called him back so that he could retrieve his favourite rings from the severed hand.

The Crimean War of 1854–56 was pretty much a fiasco all round – it was a conflict that revealed the appalling manner in which the British treated their troops. The only good thing to come out of it was fame for Florence Nightingale and Mary Seacole. The two women nursed soldiers who, before their arrival, had died in their thousands from avoidable disease and malnutrition rather than enemy action.

The Charge of the Light Brigade occurred on 25 October 1854. The Light Brigade was generally considered to be the British army's elite fighting unit at a time when ideas about the nobility of war still meant mounted soldiers were seen as the ultimate fighting machine. This despite the fact that their efficiency had long been open to question, given the invention of efficient firearms.

One of the problems was that at that time officers in the army bought their commissions – in other words, ability had nothing to do with it, and those who led the charge seem at this remove to have been fabulously dim-witted. Typically, they were officers who thought that Florence Nightingale and Mary Seacoal would make the men soft and effete.

The Earl of Lucan – ancestor of the Lucan who murdered his children's nanny in the 1970s – was Commander of the Cavalry, and the Commander of the Light Brigade was the Earl of Cardigan, who also happened to be Lucan's brother-in-law. What seems to have precipitated the decision to attack was an earlier attack by the Russians that succeeded in capturing a number of forts above Balaclava itself. This attack was halted by the British but as the Russians retreated, Raglan became concerned that they would be able to get away with their heavy guns. To prevent this he decided the Light Brigade should attack them as they retreated.

Raglan's written order still exists and it says:

> The cavalry is to advance and take advantage of any opportunity to recover the heights. They will be supported by infantry, which has been ordered. Advance on two fronts.

Lucan received the order but did not immediately execute it. Raglan was furious and sent a second order:

> Lord Raglan wishes the cavalry to advance rapidly to the front, follow the enemy, and try to prevent the enemy carrying away the guns. Troop of Horse Artillery may accompany. French cavalry is on your left. Immediate.

But Lucan had no idea what guns were referred to. He later told a Commission of Enquiry that when the officer delivering the command from Raglan was asked precisely what he, Lucan, was to attack, the young officer pointed not to the heights – which is what Ragland meant – but to the main Russian position at the foot of the Fedukhine Heights to the East. That vague arm gesture was to cost the British Army dearly.

Lucan sent the order on to Lord Cardigan, who protested that the attack would be suicide, but he was adamant: it had to go ahead and the charge began. Five cavalry divisions were involved with a total of 672 men and Cardigan led them. In less than thirty minutes almost two hundred and fifty men had been either killed or injured.

Despite these disastrous losses Lord Lucan subsequently described the event as 'a most triumphant charge . . . an attack which, for daring and gallantry, could not be exceeded'. His commanding officer Raglan tried to get Lucan court-martialled for ignoring the first order and bungling the second. In a heated debate conducted for years after the event in the pages of *The Times* Raglan insisted his order had been to attack the heights. Lucan countered by saying Nolan had been imprecise in passing on Raglan's order.

History has tended to judge Lucan as the most culpable in a hugely bungled strategy – not for ignoring the first order but for responding to a vague wave of a man's arm.

BUMP ON HEAD

INDIA, 1859

Military men are often at their maddest when they are off duty and this is no more true than during the long period in which the British ruled India. Maybe it was the permanent heat or the distance from home, but many soldiers serving with the Raj developed some very strange habits indeed.

A shortsighted old colonel on leave from the Indian Army was hunting Bengal tigers from the top of what was reputed to be the most intelligent elephant in India. The animal was famous for sensing when it was near a tiger and would wave its trunk in the right direction and stop absolutely still – like a pointer that had discovered a pheasant – whenever this happened. As they moved along a particularly narrow ride the elephant stopped dead in its tracks and waved its trunk frantically, indicating the presence of a tiger a little ahead and to the left. Moments later two tigers appeared just feet ahead of the party perched on their elephant and, before anyone could move, the bigger of the tigers launched itself at the head of the elephant and clung there for an instant.

The elephant roared and reared its head, but did not bolt or charge ahead. But the animal's bellowing and sudden shaking threw off the tiger, giving the old colonel, whose presence of mind was in marked contrast to his aged appearance, just enough time to shoot. The first bullet finished off the first tiger while the second missed its target.

All the while the mahout – the elephant's handler – had struggled to keep the elephant under control. It was assumed that his efforts in bashing the poor beast on the head with a heavy blunt instrument caused a massive swelling that appeared and grew worse over the days and weeks that followed the incident with the tiger. The elephant was so greatly liked and admired by its owners that the mahout was in danger of being sacked as the by-now massive boil showed no signs of healing and the animal was becoming increasingly distressed by the pain.

Finally the owners called in a vet, who lanced the boil while the elephant remained as quiet as a lamb. And who would have believed it? When the boil burst, out popped the second of those two .500 bullets that had been fired at the tigers!

WOODEN HAND

MEXICO, 1863

With an extraordinary history of fighting, the French Foreign Legion is traditionally seen as one of the toughest armies in the world. But their proudest moment came in Mexico when Captain Jean Danjou and just sixty-four men fought to the death at a little-known place called Camerone.

The story began when Danjou was issued with orders that he and his men were to keep open the road from Vera Cruz to Mexico City so the French could send through safely a convoy carrying gold, arms and ammunition. Having marched all night along the road, Danjou and his men made camp at a high point and waited. They did not know that the Mexican army's scouts had spotted them and decided to attack. As soon as the attack began, knowing that his position on the road would be far too difficult to defend, Danjou retreated to a farmhouse at the village of Camerone.

Danjou's plan must have been to hold out against the Mexicans until the main body of French legionnaires arrived, but he had not expected the huge army with which he quickly found himself faced. The Mexicans were estimated at three hundred cavalry, three hundred and fifty guerillas and three battalions of infantry. The situation was made even worse because in the retreat from the road to the farmhouse, sixteen Legion soldiers had already been killed or wounded, leaving only forty-eight to defend the farmhouse.

Danjou knew that it was only a matter of time before they were all slaughtered but he was determined to go down

85

fighting. It is said that he made every man swear an oath to fight to the end despite the fact that he knew they would have to fight with nothing to eat or drink, and against overwhelming odds. By six o' clock on that first evening only twelve legionnaires remained alive and uninjured – Danjou one of them. A little after six Colonel Milan, who commanded the Mexican troops, decided on an all-out attack on the barn. Even then, as the Mexicans stormed through the doors and windows, the last remaining Frenchmen were ordered to attack by their one remaining officer. They fixed bayonets and ran at their attackers out into the courtyard. All but three were immediately caught in a hail of bullets and killed.

The battle had lasted almost ten hours: twenty Frenchmen were dead, twenty badly wounded and another twenty taken prisoner. The Mexicans had lost more than three hundred men – and for nothing. During the battle the convoy had passed unscathed along the road.

Every year, in a bizarre ceremony involving a wooden hand, the French Foreign Legion remembers Danjou, who had lost a hand in an earlier action. After that final battle his wooden replacement was the only part of him to be found.

LAMENT FOR THE DEAD

AMERICA, 1862

The haunting lament played at US military funerals was first used in 1862 during the American Civil War, but its specific origins are quite extraordinary. The story begins with Union Army Captain Robert Ellicombe, who was serving at Harrison's Landing in Virginia.

After weeks of fierce fighting Ellicombe and his men were bogged down. The Confederate army against which they were pitted was dug in just a few hundred yards away across a narrow strip of no man's land. The stress and noise of battle – even at night sharp shooters kept up a steady rattle of fire – meant that most nights Ellicombe slept only fitfully and he was constantly alert to the sounds coming from the enemy side.

During a lull on hostilities, Ellicombe was sitting up alone one night when he heard the faint sounds of a wounded soldier: the man had clearly been injured in the last skirmish between the two sides.

Despite the risks Ellicombe decided to go out under cover of darkness and try to rescue the soldier. He crawled slowly across no man's land and, despite the occasional crack of gunfire, reached the stricken soldier. Miraculously, he managed to pull the injured man back to the Union lines without being hit and only then, under the faint light of a campfire, did he look at the young injured soldier's face.

He'd assumed that the soldier was a Union man and was horrified when he realised he was actually a Confederate, but imagine his horror when he looked at the young man's face and realised it was his own son! Attempts to save the young soldier were futile and minutes later he died in his father's arms. Before the war began he'd been studying music in the South and once it started he'd joined the Confederate army, but his father – hundreds of miles away – never knew.

Ellicombe knew his superiors were unlikely to grant him permission to give his son a full military funeral, but he was allowed to give his son a military funeral of sorts. The normal routine at the time was for a military band to play a lament over the grave of a fallen soldier, but this was too much for Ellicombe's superiors, given that the dead man had been fighting for the other side. Instead Ellicombe was allowed to choose a single member of the band to play a simple tune. The captain chose a bugler, who was asked to play a short piece of music that had been found on a scrap of paper in the dead soldier's pocket.

That anonymous piece of music by a soldier about whom almost nothing is known is now the famous 'Taps' tune used at all American military funerals.

BATTLE OF THE IRONCLADS

AMERICA, 1862

The world's first battle between ships clad in iron took place in America between the USS Monitor and the confederate ship Merrimack on 9 March 1862.

Merrimack was an old wooden ship that had iron plates attached to give her extra protection in battle. She had ten guns and was fixed with a fearsome-looking steel ram. Her armour plate was fitted at an angle in an attempt to make enemy shot richochet away, but the Merrimack's great disadvantage was a top speed of just a few knots, perhaps four at most.

The Monitor, on the other hand, was the pride of the Yankee navy. She'd been purpose built at huge expense and was fitted with four-inch thick steel plating. With just two guns she was seriously under-gunned, but had the supreme advantage over Merrimack in that she could travel at eight knots with ease. Monitor's guns were fitted in a heavily armoured revolving turret and she had almost certainly been built after the Union authorities heard about the Confederates' new metal-hulled ship.

The battle between the two hi-tech ships began on 8 March 1862 when the Merrimack moved out of Norfolk Virginia in an attempt to break through a blockade of five Union ships guarding the mouth of the St James River. Blasting away with her ten guns, the Merrimack quickly sank two Union ships and forced another to run aground, but she then had to beat a hasty retreat. Next day she tried again, but the Monitor was now in position.

In an almost surreal battle that lasted for two days the two ships fired at each other from virtually point blank range, but with the low velocity ammunition in use at that time they did little harm. During the battle the ships frequently collided and the appalling noise of shots hitting metal permanently deafened the sailors on board both ships.

In the end the battle proved inconclusive: a chance shot wounded the captain of the Monitor, who'd been stationed in the gun turret, and the ship temporarily withdrew; Merrimack was in a terrible state, its engines almost exhausted. The Merrimack went back into the harbour and claimed victory, but the Monitor also claimed victory as the Merrimack had gone into harbour while she, the Monitor, had only sailed a short distance away from the scene of the engagement. In truth neither side had won, a reflection of the fact that at this time it was easier to build impressive armour plating than effective ordinance.

CONFEDERATE SUBMARINE

AMERICA, 1863

Submarines don't sound like the kind of technology used in nineteenth century conflicts but they were certainly used in the American Civil War. The submarine known as the H. L. Hunley was, on a number of occasions, used by the Confederates but its contribution to the war effort was at best limited.

The H. L. Hunley was a simple iron tube, actually made from an old iron boiler, which had tapered ends bolted on to it. A small crew drove the bizarre machine using a hand cranked propeller, while a single submariner tried to steer the ship, which was almost impossible with visibility almost zero under water in the days before radar. The crew operated hand pumps to empty and fill ballast tanks, thus enabling the submarine to rise or fall in the water, and for emergencies there were detachable iron weights. If the machine got into trouble, these could be removed and the submarine would rise to the surface, whatever the state of the pumps.

In 1864 the Hunley was used with deadly effect. The USS Housatonic, an 1800-ton warship with twenty-three guns, lay at anchor in Charleston Harbour off the coast of South Carolina. Under cover of darkness the Hunley approached the warship and attacked it with a primitive torpedo made from a long pole attached to the prow of the submarine. On the end of the pole was fixed an explosive head. The head was fitted with a spike that embedded itself in the wooden side of the warship. The Hunley backed away, leaving a detonating wire attached to

91

the head of the torpedo. When they thought they were far away enough, the crew of the Hunley yanked on their wire and the torpedo exploded. But the Hunley's crew had seriously misjudged the distance they needed to be away to avoid the effects of the explosion and as a result they themselves were blown to pieces. Both the warship and the submarine sank to the bottom of Charleston Harbour! All nine members of the crew were lost, as were the five men aboard the USS Housatonic.

STONEWALL'S END

AMERICA, 1863

Born in 1824, the legendary American Civil War fighter General Stonewall Jackson was a devout – some would say crackpot – Presbyterian who, in a military career of extraordinary luck and daring, survived numerous ferocious encounters with Union armies only to die after being shot by one of his own men.

So austere a figure was Jackson that he was compared to Oliver Cromwell and referred to as 'the Deacon' by his fellow officers. When the Civil War began he had been teaching in a Military Academy but was immediately sent to organise the new Confederate Army. From the start he was in the thick of a war that was to claim tens of thousands of lives and tear America apart. Brothers from the same family fought on opposite sides and whole communities took decades to recover from their sense of loss and betrayal.

Jackson most famously led his Confederate troops in 1861 at the battle of Bull Run. A fellow general who watched him in action described him as standing against the Union soldiers 'like a stone wall'. The name stuck and Jackson was thereafter known as 'Stonewall Jackson'.

In May 1862 Jackson and his troops found themselves surrounded by one hundred and fifteen thousand Union soldiers in the Shenandoah Valley. Jackson had just seventeen thousand men. He was ordered just to do his best to slow the Union troops down – they were heading towards the town of Richmond, which had no other defences. But Jackson brilliantly and successfully harried the huge Union army before heading east to join a bigger army of Confederates led by Joseph E. Johnstone.

A year later at the James River in 1862 Jackson beat off troops sent in by Abraham Lincoln. Then, in September 1862, he fought at Antietam, where on the 17th, he held out against more than seventy-five thousand union troops with a force of just over thirty-seven thousand Confederate soldiers. After returning from the battlefield at Chancellorsville in May 1863 and after all his extraordinary escapes, often when hopelessly outnumbered, Jackson was accidentally shot by one of his own men. Though his left arm was successfully amputated he developed pneumonia and died on 10 May 1863.

OBSESSIVE ENERGY

AMERICA, 1864

One of the strangest American military leaders was John Hunt Morgan (1825–64), who came from Lexington in Kentucky. During the Civil War he joined the Confederate Army and, in April 1861, set off with a party of eight hundred soldiers. With little military experience he simply made off-the-cuff decisions about what he thought would work militarily, and in just over three weeks he and his men rode more than a thousand miles and captured nearly twelve hundred prisoners. An astonishing achievement for a man with no formal training and hardly any experience.

Two years later Morgan led another raiding party, this time against the Northern Army. He and his men slept just three hours a day and rode hard for the best part of the remainder. After more than a month of skirmishing, in July 1863, Morgan and his army were trapped on an island in the Ohio River. Forced to surrender he and his main commanders were jailed, but even here Morgan's almost obsessive energy and intuitive brilliance led to an extraordinary escape. He and his men managed to tunnel several hundred yards under the perimeter of the Columbus Jail before escaping.

A year later he was back with his raiding party in Kentucky, but his extraordinary luck finally ran out in 1864 during a raid on Tennessee. He and his normally ultra cautious troops were caught off-guard by a company of Union cavalry. They refused to surrender and were cut down in a hail of bullets.

BUFFALO SOLDIERS

AMERICA, 1866

In earlier times one of the most effective fighting forces in the American army was the roughly two hundred thousand African-American soldiers, who fought through some of the worst campaigns of the late nineteenth century and the Civil War, despite the huge discrimination they suffered from Americans of European origin.

More than thirty thousand African-American soldiers died in the Civil War alone. In the 1860s they fought in segregated units established by Congress. Two cavalry regiments – the 9th and 10th – and four infantry regiments were then given some of the hardest jobs in the US army; in fact, all-black regiments made up more than twenty per cent of frontier units. The men were also used in gruelling conditions against native Americans, rustlers and other outlaws. After battles with the various native American tribes, but particularly the Commanches and Cheyenne, the black regiments earned one of the strangest names in military history. The native Americans christened them 'buffalo soldiers. This was a mark of respect, for they fought some of the greatest of all Indian military leaders, including Lone Wolf, Sitting Bull and Geronimo, but looked like the Indians' old adversary: the buffalo that once roamed the American plains before being virtually wiped out by the Europeans.

In the 1870s the black cavalry regiments helped implement American government policy of stealing the last land owned by the Apache tribe in order to hand it over to contractors for building and mining. Under inspired leaders like Geronimo, the Apaches fought back until in 1885 the Buffalo soldiers were transferred out of the region.

ON YER BIKE!

GERMANY, 1870

The military always like to keep an eye on new inventions just to see if they might possibly have military potential, which is why the invention of the bicycle in the 1870s led to great excitement among the top brass of Europe.

Here at last was a swift and efficient means of travel that didn't require plenty of hay or oats every day and thus it was that the bicycle made its debut in war during the Franco-Prussian conflict of 1870. The generals were delighted – soldiers could move quickly and silently on their new iron steeds and carry a great deal more than they could otherwise manage on foot.

One thing they quickly discovered, however, is that soldiers who fire their rifles (or any other weapon for that matter) while riding a bicycle tend to fall off and wielding a sword is equally difficult. Kitchener was mad keen to see bicycles in action in the Boer War. He asked for a thousand cyclists for South Africa, but volunteers in Britain produced only two of the eight companies requested.

During World Wars One and Two bicycles were a significant part of the war effort despite the fact that, as one commentator observed wryly, 'They just cannot be made to look in the least war-like!'

THE LAST TO GO

FRANCE, 1870

To this day the idea that war is the proper employment for a gentleman lasts – which is why young men at Sandhurst do not generally come from poor areas of Glasgow or Salford. In earlier times war even involved kings and their aides. The last great glittering array of nobility at a battle occurred at Sedan in France in 1870 during the Franco-Prussian War.

On a high point above Frenois the Prussian king watched with Bismarck in attendance, along with Prince Leopold of Bavaria, Prince William of Wurttemburg, Duke Frederick of Schleswig-Holstein, the Duke of Saxe Coburg (a near relation of Queen Victoria), the Grand Duke of Saxe-Weimar and the Grand Duke of Mecklenburg-Strelitz. What they saw must have horrified them: wave after wave of French cavalry attacked the German lines only to be mown down by the new rapid fire breech-loading guns that had just come into use. But the absolute conviction, based on romantic attachment rather than solid reasoning, that mounted soldiers were uniquely effective even outlasted this tragic display of their uselessness for they were still seen, though on the fringes of the main theatres of war, during 1914–18.

With the battlefield at Frenois strewn with the corpses of men and animals the leader of the French cavalry rallied with other survivors and was approached by General Gallifet, who asked the immortal (or immortally stupid) question: 'Do you think you could try again?' The brave young cavalry officer, though clearly knowing it was hopeless, immediately replied,

'As often as you like.' The age of cavalry was over, but the generals and the aristocrats on their hill top did not like the idea and refused to believe it.

Again and again, they asked the diminished remains of the cavalry to charge and charge despite their dwindling numbers and sense of hopelessness. But the infantry knew it was hopeless and despite the rousing pleas of their officers they would not advance behind the cavalry. The last attack of the cavalry was the worst of all – the bloodshed was fearful – but then something extraordinary happened. As they reached the German lines Gallifet and his last few fellow cavalrymen turned, having somehow miraculously escaped the hail of bullets. As they passed along, just a few yards in front of the Germans, their guns fell silent and a German officer rose and saluted the French cavalrymen before allowing them to ride away unharmed.

GOING ROUND IN CIRCLES

RUSSIA, 1873

Ships, tanks and aeroplanes designed for war can always be improved, but what looks good on the drawing board doesn't always work in the real world – as the Russian Admiral Popov discovered in 1873. That was the year that saw the launch of one of the strangest military machines ever invented.

It was early one autumn morning that the warship Novgorod put to sea from the Black Sea port of Nikolaiev. For months rumour had been rife among the inhabitants of the town that this was to be no ordinary launch and as the ship hit the water there were gasps of astonishment. At more than two thousand five hundred tonnes the Novgorod was big for her time; she was also bristling with armaments – and perfectly circular.

Popov had been faced with a difficult design problem: he needed a warship that could operate in shallow coastal waters but he had been given a lengthy list of armaments by the Czar and was told that everything on the list had to be on the ship. The Czar, who was paranoid that his country was in danger of invasion, had put so many things on the list that a conventional warship small enough to do the work of patrolling inlets and bays would have sunk. The Novgorod was the solution. It had a shallow draught and, being circular, could achieve angles of fire from its myriad weapons that were only dreamt of on conventional warships.

Novgorod had a central tower fitted with two massive ten-ton guns that could be turned full circle. The ship was kitted out with no less than twelve powerful screw propellers and,

101

properly used, they could propel the ship forward or backward, even make it spin rapidly clockwise or anticlockwise. The sailors who manned the Novgorod reported that it was unusually stable even in rough weather.

The biggest drawback to the circular warship and the main reason only two were ever built was that they were very slow. With a top speed of about ten knots, they could never compete in open water with more conventional ships and with no keel and a very shallow draught they were incredibly difficult to steer at all. One captain reported that steering the Novgorod was like ice-skating with butter on the soles of your boots!

CUSTER BOWS OUT

AMERICA, 1876

It's no surprise really that at West Point and other US military academies the battle plans of the native Americans are still studied – they were often quite brilliant and infinitely superior to the rather leaden and hidebound tactics of the white invaders.

One of the most extraordinary battles in the long years it took the invaders to crush Indian opposition to the takeover of their country took place in 1876 at Little Big Horn in the Rocky Mountains. On 25 June the fight took place between a mixed band of Sioux and Cheyenne and General George Custer and five companies of the US seventh cavalry. In what came to be known as Custer's Last Stand, the whole of Custer's army was destroyed. The image was of a lone hero fighting against a bunch of savages, but in fact Custer was a brutal incompetent egotist attempting to destroy the indigenous people of the region.

Custer's three columns converged on the Big Horn Plains from the North West, the North East and the South East. The southern column had already been badly mauled by Crazy Horse at the Battle of the Rosebud on 17 June and as a result they slowed to a halt. Crazy Horse met Sitting Bull at the Little Big Horn Valley, where Custer's forces were headed: the idea was to complete a double encirclement.

Custer came within striking distance of the Indian encampment two days ahead of Commander Terry, who was leading the remaining US forces. Indian scouts spotted the approaching army, which meant of course that Custer lost the element of surprise. Almost certainly he should have waited, but obsessed by the idea of personal glory, he decided instead to attack immediately. The army split into three – five companies under Custer set off to the North, three companies went with Major Reno to the South and Captain Benteen went through the hills with the three remaining companies. A final company stayed behind to guard supplies.

Reno's companies were first to advance on the Indian encampment but they soon found that rather than attacking they were suddenly in a defensive position, outmanoeuvred and outnumbered. They fell back to what is now known as Reno Hill, where they held out for two days. Benteen's men arrived as Reno's were retreating, but there was little they could do other than bed down with Reno's companies at the hill. Custer's companies were all that now remained; with Reno and Benteen's men pinned down the Indians were able to concentrate on Custer and his men.

The battle had started at 1 p.m. that day. By 6 p.m. Custer was dead, along with all his men. For the Indians it was an extraordinary victory against all the odds. But of course winning one battle means nothing if you cannot win the war and in the long run, the Indians' attempts to retain even a small part of their land were doomed to failure.

FIGHTING VICAR

SOUTH AFRICA, 1879

The Zulu wars of the second half of the nineteenth century produced many acts of extraordinary bravery and foolishness, on the side of the colonialists and the Zulus alike, but there are few characters to compare with the remarkable George Smith.

An English vicar, Smith could hardly have looked less like a man of God. He was a central figure at the Battle of Rorke's Drift, where he behaved with reckless, almost suicidal, military (rather than religious) zeal. Smith weighed over twenty stone and at more than six feet six inches tall he was a terrifying sight, both to his own men and to the enemy. And rather than simply preach to the men or tend to their spiritual needs, or comfort them when they were dying, he liked to get in the thick of the action.

At the height of the battle at Rorke's Drift, Smith was seen marching up and down the defensive perimeter in full view of the enemy, handing out Martini Henry cartridges to the men. With his huge red beard and massive frame, he was a presence the men could not ignore and, when the battle grew increasingly desperate, he began to march up and down even faster with his boxes of ammunition. But by now he was also shouting and bellowing quotations from the Bible. His favourite exhortation was, 'Don't swear, boys, just shoot!' After the battle – which he survived – he was always known as 'Ammunition' Smith.

ZULU WARS

SOUTH AFRICA, 1879

At Isandhlwana Hill in South Africa in 1879 the British sense of imperial destiny and invincibility was dealt a crushing, and frankly astonishing, blow.

A huge force of British soldiers left Natal on 11 January 1879 with the aim of pushing the Zulus out of their strongholds west of the Buffalo River. More than eighteen companies began the march, crossing the river and heading up on to the Nqutu plateau. So many troops were involved that it took them a whole day to cross the river at a place that was to become famous or infamous throughout the British Empire: it was called Rorke's Drift.

The troops camped on the other side of the river while roadways were improved with stones and gravel for the wagons moving up behind. Seven days later on 20 January the wagons and troops had advanced just fifteen miles to a place called Isandhlwana Hill. Here, they made camp but fatally for them, and against all regulations, they did not construct fortifications.

On 22 January forward patrols met a large body of Zulus. Reinforcements were brought up immediately as the British officers assumed this was the main body of Zulus, but what they didn't know was that the main body of some twenty thousand warriors was hidden in a ravine six miles away. The Zulus were waiting partly because the night of the 22nd was a full moon – an ill-omen – but when their position was discovered by a British scout they quickly formed up for an attack. Astonishingly they ran the six miles to the British front line, which they reached at around midday.

Almost from the start the British realised that in not building fortifications they had made a terrible and stupid mistake. For the first couple of hours they held their own against wave after wave of Zulu warriors but ammunition ran low and re-supply was poor. Soon the weight of numbers began to tell until the centre of the British line collapsed and the Zulus surged through to encircle the remaining British troops, all of whom were killed.

Just a few dozen British soldiers escaped and lived to tell the tale. For the British it was an astonishing blow – a huge army defeated by people considered at the time to be no match for the might of Empire.

THE MAD MADHI

The idea of Islamic fundamentalism is not a new one by any means. In the past powerful Islamic figures have occasionally decided that their interpretation of Islam is the only correct one and anyone who disagrees with them can be killed with the blessing of Allah.

One such was the Mahdi, a radical Islamic leader generally held, by the British at least, to be responsible for the death of Victorian hero Charles 'Chinese' Gordon at Khartoum in 1885. Between 1881–85 the Mahdi did everything in his power to create what he called a pure Islamic state, much to the disgust of the British who, in turn, did everything they could to be rid of him.

Today many Islamic fundamentalists still see him as the father of independence and as a great and holy Islamic figure, neatly ignoring the fact that when he died, sprawled in his hareem, he was hugely bloated from overeating. The Mahdi, or Messiah as he modestly liked to think of himself, was born Mohammed Ahmed-Ibn-el-Sayed in 1844 at Dongola, Sudan. His father claimed to be a direct descendant of the Prophet Mohammed. As a young adult he moved to Abba, about one hundred and fifty miles from Khartoum, and began a lifestyle that is common among the very religious: he fasted until he had hallucinations that he interpreted as the prophet talking to him. Almost inevitably he attracted a group of disciples, who loved his claims that the prophet had revealed to him that paradise awaited the poor of Sudan above all others.

The Mahdi came to prominence in 1881 when he called for all true believers to rise in jihad – or holy war – against their Christian – British – rulers. Thousands answered the call and in 1883 they scored their first huge success in slaughtering a British army of eleven thousand strong. Unusually for the time, the British decided to abandon Upper Egypt but that meant a huge evacuation of civilian men and women, and soldiers. Thousands of Europeans had taken refuge in Khartoum and other towns and the British government was convinced that only one person was up to the job of sorting out the mess. That person was General Gordon and in January 1884 he was directed to superintend the evacuation.

Within a month of his arrival at Khartoum, Gordon had successfully evacuated thousands of women and children, but thousands remained and, while he was still negotiating, the Mahdi and his men suddenly attacked. Gordon wrote of this time: 'Our only justification for assuming the offensive is the extrication of Halfaya, where eight hundred men are garrisoned'.

When Gordon's men tried to begin the exodus the Mahdi's army cut off three companies of his troops and killed more than a hundred men. They then dug in all along the Nile and fired at any British troop boats that tried to pass along the river. For the garrison retreat was impossible, the river being the only way. Gordon decided that grain barges, fitted with steel plate and heavy guns, towed by steamer were the answer. They successfully ran the gauntlet of the militias on the banks of the Nile and eventually managed to extricate the remaining men from the garrison.

Halfaya was taken by the Mahdi and from then on Gordon's attempts to defend Khartoum grew steadily more desperate. His major difficulty was that he had to rely on what were then known as native troops and as he himself said at one point, there was no way to know when the next group would desert and join the Mahdi.

For months, desultory battles ensued between the Mahdi's forces and Gordon's men. Most were conducted along the Nile, this being the only route in and out of the country at that time. Gradually Gordon's position was weakened. Though he tried negotiating with the Mahdi, this failed after Gordon apparently rejected the idea of becoming a Muslim!

Gordon did his utmost to organise Khartoum in such a way that it could be defended indefinitely but the lack of trust-worthy troops – he had absolutely none – made this extremely difficult. As one independent reporter wrote at the time: 'Five hundred brave men could have cleared out the lot [the Mahdi's besieging forces] but he had not a hundred in a war strange like no other in history'.

Early in 1884 Gordon telegraphed to say that he had provisions for five months and that with two or three thousand troops he could soon settle the rebels. Unfortunately, not one soldier was sent to help him. Gradually more and more towns fell into the hands of the Mahdi. Gordon mined the area around Khartoum; he used land mines, barbed wire and every other expedient to delay the end but he must have known it was not far off. By April 1884 Gordon was entirely cut off from the outside world, but still his steamers were sent up the Nile to shell the Mahdi's positions and to gather food. Time was running out, however.

In the centre of Khartoum Gordon built a defensive tower and kept a lookout from it day and night. Treachery was always his greatest fear because huge numbers of Khartoum's citizens sympathised with the Mahdi and his aims. But by now there was talk of a relief force being on its way. Gordon's spirits were said to have been hugely revived by this news – he 'rejoiced exceedingly' reported one of his aides.

But on 14 December Gordon wrote a letter to a friend saying, 'Farewell, you will never hear from me again. I fear that there will be treachery in the garrison, and all will be over by Christmas'. And so it was. On 26 January 1885 Faraz Pasha, one of Gordon's lieutenants, opened the gates of the city to the enemy and one of the most famous sieges in the world's history came to a close. It had lasted from 12 March to 26 January – exactly three hundred and twenty days.

Gordon woke to hear that his Egyptian lieutenant had betrayed him and that Khartoum was in the hands of the Mahdi. But he still set out to walk across the city, which was his daily habit. He was recognised by a party of rebels and shot. Amid the wild rejoicings of the Mahdi's followers Gordon's head was carried at the end of a pike through the town. Two days later the English army of relief reached Khartoum.

JACKAL SNAPPER

INDIA, 1890

A British Naval ship was riding at anchor in the Hooghli River some miles downstream from Calcutta. One of the ship's young officers decided he would go jackal shooting along the banks of one of the tributaries of the sacred river Ganges, a place where it was known that these wild dogs came down to eat and drink. Mostly what they ate were the bodies of the drowned, which tended to be swept ashore in one particular place, and it was to this place that the young officer went early one morning in 1890.

The young officer had shot several wild dogs when he came across a very young jackal puppy. He didn't have the heart to shoot it so he looked around for some way to take it back to the ship with him. Nothing could be found, so he took off his belt and tied it round the young jackal's neck. At that very instant the man was struck by the tail of a huge alligator, which had virtually thrown itself up the gravel bank. He fell on his face in about eighteen inches of water, but in the very act of falling he swung the puppy, which was still at the end of his belt, into the river. The poor animal was instantly snapped up by the alligator and devoured wholesale – even the young man's belt and buckle vanished into its maw.

Later the sailor admitted he was extremely lucky that the puppy had taken the edge off the alligator's appetite long enough for him to drag himself out of the water and away from danger.

GUN SURPRISE

AFRICA, 1891

The number of stories of extraordinary coincidences that are being discussed, told and re-told across the world at any one time would fill a book. But, as an eminent statistician once said: 'When you have a world with nine billion people in it I think it would be true to say that if we did not have a relatively large number of coincidences that in itself would be a greater coincidence than the ones we find so astonishing.'

Despite these rational explanations one military coincidence that really takes the biscuit concerned a soldier fighting in the French Army towards the end of the nineteenth century. Captain Battreau was old enough to have fought in the Franco German War of 1870 using what was known as a standard issue Chassepot rifle, serial number 187017. At the end of that conflict he had to hand the gun in but, like most soldiers who are taught that while they are in the army their rifle is their most important asset, he never forgot the serial number.

More than twenty years later in 1891 a much older Captain Battreau found himself still in the French Army and fighting in the Dahomey jungle in the African state of Benin. Battreau was now a highly experienced officer in the French Foreign Legion, and at the end of one particularly savage bout of hand-to-hand fighting he managed to disarm an enemy soldier. To his utter astonishment he discovered that the soldier was carrying the very same Chassepot rifle he had handed in all those years ago at the end of the 1870 campaign.

HILL-TOP COCK-UP

SOUTH AFRICA, 1900

During the Second Boer War (1899–1902) the British army became involved in one of the oddest, most incompetent battles in a war that seems strange in almost every respect by modern standards. Like so many military engagements it was messy and muddled in the extreme, but it was messy in pursuit of colonial ideals that now seem almost incomprehensible.

It was January 1900 and the British decided they would attack Spionkop, a high peak twenty-one miles from Ladysmith in Natal. They decided to move at night in order to take the strategically important top of the hill, which would enable them to outflank the Boers. The British moved off quickly after dark, found the hill-top was defended by only a relatively small number of Boers and quickly defeated them. They must have heartily congratulated themselves, but first light brought the realisation that they'd gone halfway up the hill and stopped, thinking they'd reached the summit, which they most assuredly had not. The true peak – now only a short distance above the British – was heavily defended and in the real conflict that now took place, the British losses were huge.

Farce took over. Against the odds the British fought hard, but at the very moment when they decided to abandon the hill, the Boers decided to make a run for it, too. But being the first to realise that the other side had given up, the Boers quickly turned round and re-took the hill. The British must have been kicking themselves.

BARKING BARON

When, in 1908, King Edward VII presented Lieutenant General Baron Rudolf von Slatin with the silver star of the knighthood Royal Victorian Order, he became Europe's most titled and most decorated soldier.

Indeed, so weighed down was he with medals and honours that the King could not find a spot on his chest to pin his latest honour. Astonished at the array of medals stretched across the great man's chest, the King merely remarked: 'Why don't you turn around and I'll pin it to your back?'

Born in 1857 the son of a silk dyer in Vienna, von Slatin was an Austrian baron, an Eqyptian Pasha and a British knight. At one time or another, he had been decorated by virtually every European head of state including the Pope! He was a personal friend of Queen Victoria – 'What a strange, delightful little man!' she is reported to have said of him.

Aged seventeen von Slatin had set out for Cairo, where he worked in a bookshop. Fascinated by General Gordon of Khartoum he contrived to get a job on the great man's general staff. When he returned to Austria to do his national army service, he astonished his superiors and fellow officers by producing a letter of recommendation from General Gordon, who by that time was famous across Europe – after that von Slatin's rise was meteoric.

Back in the Sudan where he'd served under General Gordon, von Slatin became Governor General of Dar Fur Province. When his soldiers told him he could not hope to defeat the rebellious Muslim leader Mahdi, he promptly became a Muslim and defeated the rebel leader. After his conversion, Gordon – who'd been a great admirer of von Slatin – refused ever to speak to him again, largely because he was a fanatical Christian.

Meanwhile von Slatin organised his own hareem and lived like a traditional Muslim. When Gordon was killed during a later uprising von Slatin surrendered to the new Muslim government and was treated fairly well, although he was effectively held captive for the next twelve years. His only complaint was that the new government, for which he worked tirelessly, would only pay him in women, not money!

In 1895 British Intelligence whisked von Slatin away by camel to Aswan. After living like a desert Arab for so long he was apparently unrecognisable; once washed and shaved he entered the British officer's mess to a tumultuous reception and was soon the most celebrated man in Europe.

He wrote a book about his time in the desert called *Fire and Sword* and dedicated it to Queen Victoria. It became a bestseller; he was also awarded the Order of St Michael and St George and the Order of the Bath. In 1899 Emperor Franz Josef made him a knight of the Austro-Hungarian Empire; then in 1906 he was made a Baron, and from 1900–14 he held the post of Inspector General of the Sudan.

When World War One began von Slatin offered his services to the local British consul before setting off to work for the Austrian Red Cross. But then, when the war ended, he was astonished to be told he was no longer welcome in London as he'd worked for the enemy. He was also forbidden to wear his British decorations, or to use his double knighthood. Refusing to give up, he wrote endless letters to King George V and Lord Curzon until, in 1927, worn out by the indefatigable little man, the British government gave in and let him return. In 1932 he was received at Buckingham Palace, but was told that he should not, under any circumstances, turn up wearing his vast array of military and other decorations.

NEARLY SHOT

WILTSHIRE, 1913

The Great War was sparked off by the assassination of Archduke Franz Ferdinand of Austria, but history might have been very different if the Archduke had not had a narrow escape on the English shooting field just a year earlier when he'd been a guest of the Duke of Portland.

Like virtually every landowner in Edwardian Britain, the sixth Duke of Portland was a keen shot, but he was also well connected right across Europe and frequently had foreign Heads of State to stay. He tended to mix these with a liberal sprinkling of kings and princes. It was not uncommon to find that the group of guests at a Portland shooting day some crisp November in 1913 consisted, as it did on one well documented occasion, of King Carlos of Portugal, the King of Spain and Archduke Franz Ferdinand of Austria, among others. Portland always ranked his guests in order of shooting ability – whether or not they were good company was quite irrelevant – and Franz Ferdinand apparently took pride of place as a marksman, with Portugal second and Spain third. It took the Archduke just a few days to get used to the high flying pheasants so beloved of the English aristocracy – Ferdinand was actually an expert rifleman – and after their first week together Portland pronounced him, 'certainly the equal of most of my friends'.

Then, in December, the Archduke was shooting, along with a mixed European bag of guests, on a day of deep snow. He was shooting with two loaders, one of whom slipped and fell. The gun the man was carrying went off as it hit the ground and both

117

barrels were discharged, the shot passing within a foot of the Archduke's head.

For years afterwards the Duke of Portland would say to anyone who would listen, 'I have often wondered if the Great War might not have been averted, or at least postponed, had the Archduke met his death then, and not at Sarajevo in the following year.'

THE GHOST SHIP

CHILE, 1913

The Marie Celeste is, of course, the most famous of all ghost ships but she is by no means alone – many other ships have vanished only to be discovered years later, apparently still more or less sea-worthy, yet entirely unmanned. Even when there is no real reason to think that some kind of malevolent supernatural influence is at work, the discovery of a floating hulk with all its gear more or less intact and yet not a man aboard is enough to make the most convinced sceptic nervous.

A British naval ship cruising the coastline of Chile in 1913 made a discovery that the captain never forgot. Long after he'd retired he still thought of the discovery with a cold shudder. His ship had been on the lookout for suspicious trading vessels that might be involved in smuggling or worse, when the lookout spotted a large sailing cargo ship moving slowly but under full sail. Her sails were tattered and filthy, but they were by no means ineffective and though she seemed weather beaten, her condition was certainly not enough to arouse more than a mild suspicion that this ragged craft might be up to no good.

The captain of the British naval ship decided, almost as a matter of routine, to investigate but he expected to find nothing more than the usual band of harmless South American sailors aboard. He asked the helmsman to get close to the sailing ship. After several attempts to make contact using various signals the baffled captain gave the order to board. Three men swung over the treacherous sea to the strange sailing ship but returned as quickly as they'd gone and from their faces the captain could tell that something was dreadfully amiss.

By this time other members of the navy ship's crew had noticed a number of curious things about the sailing ship: her masts and sails, for example, were covered in a thick green moss-like substance and wherever they looked along her deck they could see no sign of life. The crew could have all been below deck but a sailing ship needs continual work to keep her on course and that work has to be carried out on deck, so the apparent absence of human life was odd to say the least.

The captain ordered a boarding party back on to the sailing ship and this time they searched more carefully. They discovered the skeleton of a man lying beneath the helm; a dozen more skeletons were found in the forward hold and seven on the ship's bridge. There were no signs of violence or a struggle of any kind. Each skeleton was dressed in the tattered rags that had once been clothes. It was only when the boarding party cleared the green slime from the side of the sailing ship's prow that they could make out her name: she was the Marlborough Glasgow and back in port the captain of the naval vessel was able to uncover her strange story.

The Marlborough Glasgow had left the port of Littleton in New Zealand more than twenty years earlier in 1890. She had a crew of twenty-three and was carrying a cargo of wool and mutton. Captain Hird was in command. She should have arrived back in port a few weeks later but was never heard of again, at least that is until 1913. Towards the end of 1890 search parties went out to look for her, but found nothing and it was assumed she'd been lost in a storm with all hands.

Her discovery in 1913 caused a sensation, but how she managed to drift for twenty-three years without being overwhelmed by storms or driven on to rocks or sandbanks is a mystery that will never be solved. Tests on the crew revealed nothing about how they died; the fact that they lay in groups together suggests that whatever overwhelmed them did so incredibly quickly.

Equally bizarre was the Dundee Star, a Scottish ship abandoned by her crew during a ferocious storm off Midway

Island in the North Pacific. Having left her to the elements the crew watched helplessly as she was driven out to sea, but four years later, having been blown who knows where about the world's ocean, she was found becalmed off the very island where she'd been abandoned!

TALL STORY

ENGLAND, 1914

Stories of underage boys joining up during World War One are legion but there are equally extraordinary tales of undersized boys doing their utmost to get into the army.

Private John Singleton of the 7th Sherwood Foresters is a case in point – he made several attempts to join the regular army but each time he was turned down on the grounds that, at just five foot, he was too short. In the early part of the Great War the minimum accepted height was five foot three inches and this was not reduced to five foot until heavy losses created a need for more desperate recruiting measures.

Critics of the war were in a tiny despised minority during 1914 and men who were unable to join for one reason or another were often ostracised. Private Singleton's reaction to his failure is not therefore surprising. In an interview he explained the situation and his solution:

> My four brothers had all joined up and I was very ashamed not to be in the army. So I went to the Territorial Army Drill Hall in Derby Road, Nottingham, and offered the recruiting Sergeant there, a two shilling postal order if he would accept me. He did so, and when it was over and I'd signed up, we both went along to the local pub, cashed the postal order and drank the proceeds. My wife was working in the shell factory at the time and when she came home I told her I had joined up.

CONTEMPTIBLE KAISER

FRANCE, 1914

One of the most famous groups of war veterans in the world is the Old Contemptibles, the name given to World War One's British Expeditionary Force. But why such an apparently insulting name?

Well, the name was originally meant as a term of abuse, but the British soldiers turned it on its head and adopted it as their own. The story began when, in August 1914, Kaiser Wilhelm II ordered General von Kluck, who commanded the German First Army, to 'exterminate the treacherous English and walk over General French's contemptible little army'.

The word 'contemptible' struck the British soldiers as hilarious rather than insulting and they decided to get their revenge on the Kaiser, who was universally despised despite being closely related to the British Royal family, by adopting the insult as if it was the finest compliment. And thus were the Old Contemptibles born.

POINTLESS HUMILIATION

FRANCE, 1914

The writer and poet Robert Graves recorded in *Goodbye To All That* – his memoirs of service in the Great War – the curious traditions of the officers' mess. New officers were treated appallingly badly as part of a bizarre initiation period: they weren't allowed to drink whisky though older officers were and they were treated with open contempt by the most senior officers of all.

On Graves' first night in the mess an officer known as Buzz Off spotted him sitting quietly with a fellow new recruit at the far end of the table. Buzz Off immediately addressed the officer next to him, but in a voice loud enough for Graves and pretty much every other officer to hear:

'Who are those two funny ones down there, Charley?'

'New this morning from the militia,' came the answer. 'Answer to the names of Robertson and Graves.'

'Which is which?'

'I'm Roberston,' said Graves' friend.

'I wasn't asking you,' said the Colonel.

The Colonel then addressed Graves, rudely calling him 'Wart' and loudly asking why he was wearing his regimental stars on his shoulder instead of his sleeve. Graves replied, 'It was a regimental order in the Welsh regiment. I understood that it was the same everywhere in France.'

Graves was then told to report to the regimental master tailor and to get his uniform sorted out. The whole episode was merely an attempt, a successful one as even Graves admitted, to humiliate young officers. He was so angry that he said under his breath, 'You damned snobs – I'll survive you all! There will come a time when there won't be one of you left serving in the battalion to remember battalion mess at Laventie.'

And Graves was right. Within a year they were all dead, but he survived the war and lived into old age.

TANK TRAP

FRANCE, 1914

Fleurs-Courcelette in France saw the first use ever in warfare of the metal elephant – the tank – a British invention that military chiefs hoped would make all the difference to what was to prove a long and costly war. Initially the generals were no doubt delighted as they watched eighteen of these splendid new war machines heading off into battle, but their effectiveness was to prove short-lived.

Two of the British tank commanders were directed towards a particularly strong point in the German trenches and obediently they turned their massive vehicles in the appropriate direction. The effect on the front-line German troops, who clearly had never seen anything like these huge metal monsters before, was astonishing.

After crossing the German front line the forward of the two tanks ground to a halt while the other one managed to get into a German trench, but then couldn't get out again. But what looked like disaster quickly turned to huge success when the tank commander decided that the only thing he could do was to start firing his front mounted six-pounder gun. When he looked cautiously around for anything obvious to fire at, he noticed something quite astonishing: an acre of ground ahead of him appeared to have turned completely white! In fact, what he saw was more than four hundred German troops holding aloft anything and everything white they could lay their hands on. The only thing whiter than the handkerchiefs and other odd bits of material were the Germans' faces. Clearly, they were completely overawed by the new fighting machines and had no idea that they'd come to the end of the road.

The crew of the two tanks found themselves in an awkward position with more than four hundred prisoners suddenly in their care. By the time the four hundred realised the two tanks menacing them were actually stuck in the mud it was too late and they were being marched off to captivity.

TRUCE

FRANCE, 1914

Tales of Christmas football matches between British troops on the front line and their German counterparts during World War One have often been dismissed as myths cooked up long after the war was over to add to the sense of its futility. But a first-hand account by Captain Sir Edward Hulse proves they really did happen. He explained that when the guns fell silent on Christmas morning 1914, small groups from the German and British trenches ventured tentatively out into no man's land and by lunchtime they were exchanging jokes and organising football matches. Years later he also wrote of the extraordinary negotiations that took place on his part of the line:

> At 8.30 a.m. (on Christmas morning) I was looking out and saw four Germans leave their trenches and come towards us. I told two of my men to go and meet them unarmed as the Germans were unarmed and to see that they did not pass the halfway line.
>
> We were 350–400 yards apart at this time. My fellows were not very keen, not knowing what was up, so I went out alone and met Barry, one of our ensigns, also coming out from another part of the line. By the time we got to them they were three quarters of the way over and much too near our barbed wire so I moved them back.
>
> They were three private soldiers and a stretcher-bearer and their spokesman started off by saying that he thought

it only right to come over and wish us a happy Christmas and trusted us implicitly to keep the truce. I asked them what orders they had from their officers as to coming over to us and they said none; they had just come over out of goodwill.

We parted after an exchange of Albany cigarettes and German cigars and I went straight to headquarters to report. On my return at 10 a.m. I was surprised to hear a hell of a din going on and not a single man left in my trenches. They were completely denuded – against my orders – and nothing lived. I heard strains of 'Tipperary' floating down the breeze swiftly followed by a tremendous burst of 'Deutchsland Uber Alles', and, as I got to my own company headquarters, I saw to my amazement not only a crowd of about one hundred and fifty British and Germans at the halfway house, which I had appointed opposite my lines, but six or seven such crowds all the way down our lines and extending towards the eighth division on our right.

I bustled out and asked if there were any German officers in my crowd and the noise died down. I found two but had to talk to them through an interpreter, as they could neither talk English nor French. I explained to them that strict orders must be maintained as to meeting halfway, and everyone unarmed, and we both agreed not to fire until the other did, thereby creating a complete deadlock and armistice.

Meanwhile Scots and Huns were fraternising in the most genuine possible manner. Every sort of souvenir was exchanged, addresses given and received, photos of families shown, etc. During the afternoon, one of the enemy told me he was longing to get back to London. I assured him that so was I. He said he was sick of the war, and I told him that when the truce was ended any of his friends would be welcome in our trenches and would be well received, fed and given a free passage to the Isle of Man. The Border Regiment were occupying this section on Christmas Day and Giles Loder, our adjutant, went down there with a party that morning, on hearing of the friendly demonstrations in front of my company, to see if he could come to an agreement about our dead, who were still lying out between the trenches.

He found an extremely pleasant and superior stamp of German officer, who arranged to bring all our dead to the halfway line. We took them over there and buried twenty-nine. They apparently treated our prisoners well and did all they could for our wounded. When George heard of it, he went down to that section and talked to the nice officer and gave him a scarf. That same evening, a German orderly came to the halfway line and brought a pair of warm woolly gloves as a present in return for George.

OLD GLASS EYE

ENGLAND, 1914

Anyone who enjoys war must be mad – that would be the modern judgement on the battle hungry – but in earlier times the world took a very different view of those addicted to the art of war. As late as the 1914–18 conflict there were one or two extraordinary individuals who, despite the horrors of the trenches, still appeared to find the whole thing, if not fun, then at least utterly compelling.

Adrian Carton de Wiart seems to have been one of those soldiers who was so addicted to the ritual of war that he found its risks almost added to the interest. He'd fought in East Africa during the early part of the Great War but lost an eye and was sent home as an invalid, his war apparently over. Most soldiers, having received an honourable discharge after suffering such an injury, would accept that they had done their bit and retire gracefully – not so, de Wiart.

After relaxing for a short while he presented himself at the medical board and asked to be sent to France to fight in the trenches. The members of the board were understandably surprised at his appearance and told him that as he had only one eye they really would be able to find little use for him. He was outraged and argued with them at length. Eventually, no doubt exasperated, the board told him that if he went away and got himself a good and realistic-looking glass eye they would consider his request again.

De Wiart immediately went off to an occulist and found the best and brightest glass eye he could. Unfortunately, he also found it extremely uncomfortable but he returned to the medical board proudly wearing it and, to the astonishment of all (except de Wiart), he was accepted again for military service.

He later wrote: 'On emerging from the medical board I called a taxi, threw my glass eye out of the window, put on my black patch and have never worn a glass eye since!'

CUPBOARD LOVE

FRANCE, 1914

It is not often that a wardrobe becomes a remarkable military artefact but at least one is now in a museum, having contributed to one of the most bizarre military events in the Great War.

Trooper Patrick Fowler of the 11th Hussars managed to get trapped behind enemy lines and to avoid detection by the Germans he hid for months in a wardrobe! The story began in 1914. During fighting at Le Cateau Fowler was separated from his regiment. Having wandered aimlessly for several hours he was rescued by a middle-aged Frenchwoman, Madame Belmont-Gobert.

Madame Belmont-Gobert owned an old rambling farmhouse and in one of the sitting rooms there was a heavy old wardrobe, more of a cupboard really as it was only about five feet high, but here Trooper Fowler hid during daylight hours. Having had the run of the farmhouse for at least part of each day, he found himself in serious trouble when, after a few weeks, German troops were billeted on the farmhouse.

The Germans spent much of the day lounging about and chatting in the very room in which Trooper Fowler crouched in his wardrobe. Yet still, against all the odds, he escaped detection. Madame Belmont-Gobert was then told she would have to move out of the farmhouse into a nearby cottage, but the German soldiers agreed to help her carry her furniture, including the old wardrobe. They must have been astonished at the weight of the big old piece of country furniture, little realising that inside it, even as they carried it across the fields, sat a British soldier.

It was only when Allied troops re-occupied the village towards the end of 1918 that Fowler emerged. Madame Belmont-Gobert was decorated for her bravery as she might well have been shot by the Germans if she'd been discovered concealing a British soldier.

WARRING AT SIXTY-FIVE

AFRICA, 1914

Frederick Courtenay Selous was born in 1851 and died in 1917. From the age of six he was an obsessive hunter, shooter, butterfly and bird collector. He lived at a time when Europe and Africa seemed to have an inexhaustible supply of game and from the start he was determined to shoot and stuff as much of it as possible.

At his first school Selous lay on the hard floorboards with just a blanket so he would get used to the hardships of the hunting field. He was continually at war with the masters at Rugby School because he was never there. When he should have been at lessons he was out collecting eggs and butterflies, or shooting duck, geese, gulls – anything and everything he could. He once travelled fifteen miles late in the evening to a famous heronry where he stripped off, swam across a freezing lake, climbed a sixty-foot tree and helped himself to two eggs. Though he was back in school by morning, the eggs were confiscated until the masters learned of his efforts to get them and they were so impressed they returned the eggs to him.

On another occasion, while shooting with a number of aristocrats in Germans, he was about to lose a duck he'd shot that had fallen into the swiftly flowing Rhine. His fellow shots looked on in astonishment as he stripped off and dived into the river, swimming around ice floes to retrieve his bird.

Selous's parents sent him to Africa, where his most extraordinary day's shooting took place. In one day he shot twenty-two elephants and collected seven hundred pounds of ivory from them. Now such destruction seems indefensible but at that time it would never have occurred to anyone that African game might one day be threatened with extinction.

On sighting an elephant Selous would instantly remove his trousers as he found it easier to pursue them in his underpants and, as his London rifle was stolen when he arrived in Africa, he simply bought a local four-bore and used that instead. It was apparently a terrible gun that kicked violently and was in constant danger of exploding. Not only this, it was also almost impossible to lift, weighing in at nearly twenty pounds! Selous may have felt a slight pang about the amount of game – lions, rhinos and tigers – he shot in Africa for, in the books he later wrote, he paints endlessly vivid pictures of the sheer abundance of African game in his day.

Out shooting or not, Selous's diet consisted almost entirely of moose fat and very strong tea. He found that this combination gave him strength and courage. At camp his tea was left boiling and stewing all day and it was the evening cup he loved best. Once, while staying in a London hotel, he tested his rifle by firing at a chimneystack on the other side of the street. As he left the hotel he confided to several people in the crowd of alarmed neighbours that the sound appeared to come from the rooms above.

When he died Selous had collected thousands of birds and butterflies from all over Europe and Africa. He'd shot dozens of examples of every big game animal in the world but when in 1914 retirement loomed at the age of sixty-three, he volunteered for military service. While leading his company against a force of Germans four times the size in East Africa he was killed at the age of sixty-five.

ANIMALS AT THE FRONT

FRANCE, 1915

Between 1914 and 1917 all across the Western Front pheasants and partridges flourished, where soldiers from Britain, France and Germany died in their tens of thousands. Soldiers reported seeing pheasants and partridges carrying on with their lives completely unconcerned as all around them 5.9s and eighteen-pound shells burst. When they weren't perched on a broken stump of a tree in the middle of no man's land, they could be found grazing gently across the shell-pocked ground; and close up against the firing line soldiers frequently disturbed hares on their forms. Bizarre though the whole thing sounds it actually made sense from the creatures' point of view. The closer they were to the front, the better the feeding because the ground was constantly being churned and turned by explosives throwing up good things to eat.

One January night in 1915 a young officer wandered into a dugout with which he was unfamiliar and there, quite by chance, met a man he'd known at home in Ireland. The two men had shot together at home so they decided to try for a few pheasants the following day as they were not temporarily in the front line trenches, but some way back from them. The two were able to muster two 28-bore walking stick shotguns and they took with them one of the men's batmen, who carried a service rifle and two sandbags.

It was misty the next day when they set off – perfect conditions, given that the whole thing would have been impossible on a clear day as the Germans would have been able to see them and they'd have been quickly shot by snipers. They reached a field a little behind the front line trenches, where they had seen birds feeding. The field still had tobacco plants growing in it from earlier days during peacetime and the only difficulty was the large number of unexploded German shells littering the ground. As they walked across the field they put up several pheasants, a few partridges and snipe. They bagged a few, then noticed the Germans had clearly heard the shots and assumed there was a battery in the area for, seconds later, the air was filled with the sound of screaming shells heading toward the two sportsman and their beater. They decided to beat a hasty retreat before they were bagged by the Germans.

WAR SONG

FRANCE, 1915

It's hardly surprisingly that there are as many moving and poignant, not to say strange, stories from the Germans who fought in the Great War as from the allies. One of the most remarkable comes from the memoirs of Herbert Sulzbach, who was serving on the Western Front in August 1915.

It was well after dark when a soldier came up to one of the officers with whom Sulzbach was standing and said, 'Sir, it's that Frenchie over there, singing again so wonderfully.' Sulzbach and the other officers immediately stepped up out of their dugout into the open part of the trench and heard it – a marvelous clear tenor voice singing an aria from 'Rigoletto'.

Such was the beauty of the singing that the whole company stood absolutely still, listening intently, while it lasted. When the unknown Frenchman had finished the German soldiers cheered and applauded so loudly that a few hundred yards across no man's land the Frenchman must have heard them.

SPORTING BULGARS

SERBIA, 1915

During the Serbian battles of World War One, Bulgarian soldiers had a terrible reputation among the allies: they seemed to be brutal, torture-loving beasts. It was said that French soldiers who fell into their hands were slowly tortured to death and that they would encourage soldiers to surrender and then bayonet them.

But a young officer who met a young, captured Bulgarian soldier discovered that things looked very different from his side. The Bulgarians' German allies led them to believe that if captured by the British they would be eaten alive, a fact that was apparently widely believed and might well explain the Bulgarians' tendency to kill and ask questions later.

But at the Battle of Yenikoj a very different side to the Bulgars was seen and the British soldiers who took part were as amazed as anyone . . . British troops had all but taken the village when the Bulgarians counter attacked and established a toe-hold on the edge of the built-up area. The two sides – British and Bulgars – were no more than one hundred yards apart and firing almost continuously at each other. As one of those who took part later said: 'bullets were bouncing off absolutely everything – it was crazy.'

As the firing grew in intensity the British noticed that two of their men were lying wounded, halfway between the concealed Bulgars and their own position. They had to be brought in. Three British soldiers ran out into the open to attempt to do this, fully expecting to be met by a hail of deadly fire from the

Bulgarians. Astonishingly, as soon as the men ran into the open the Bulgarians stopped firing completely: but only at the one point where the British wounded lay. All along the rest of the line bullets continued to fly. The wounded men were brought in safely and their rescuers remained unscathed – they would almost certainly have been killed or at least badly injured if the Bulgarians had not stopped firing and allowed the rescue to take place.

Another incident that occurred – recorded by A. Donovan Young – during the same campaign revealed once again that stereotypes about the cruelty of the enemy are often wrong. Young was on outpost duty at a place called Topalova. Immediately in front of his position a troop of yeomen were in position busily firing at Bulgarian troops some way off and also in fixed positions.

The enemy still held the town of Prtosenik, which lay a few hundred yards farther off. The yeoman had just dismounted when a Bulgarian shell fell very close and terrified the horses, one of which bolted. Immediately a young soldier jumped on another horse and, forgetting the enemy was watching and that he was well within range of their guns, he set off in pursuit of the first animal.

The chase was fast, furious and enthralling. Within seconds the whole of the yeoman troop, as well as back-up infantry, were watching spellbound from the top of their parapets and in full view of the enemy. Had they wanted to do so, the Bulgarians, who employed very good snipers, could have picked off a number of British servicemen and yet nothing happened while the chase continued.

Donovan Young later recalled that he looked up and noticed the whole of the Bulgarian garrison at Ptrosenik hadn't fired because they, too, were up on their parapets watching the enthralling chase! Minutes later the trooper caught up with the runaway horse and gently trotted him back to the British lines and still not a single shot was fired. The Bulgars clearly didn't want to spoil a fine bit of sport.

MESSAGE

SERBIA, 1916

Throughout the conflict in Serbia during World War One a bizarre tradition arose whereby British and Bulgarian soldiers would leave messages pinned to trees in each others' sectors, or as the line moved forwards and then backwards.

At one stage dozens of messages were being pinned up all over the place: very few denigrated the other side; instead they were often humorous or teasing. One of the funniest message exchanges – and remember these were deadly enemies – came when the British left a message on a particular tree only to find the next morning that the enemy had pulled down the British message and left the following reply. It said: 'For goodness sake, Englishmen – write in English next time! Your French is awful!'

LIONS LED BY DONKEYS

FRANCE, 1916

Among the most extraordinary aspects of a military offensive that saw a concentration of heroism rarely seen in the history of warfare, the behaviour of the Newfoundland Regiment stands out as almost unbearably heroic.

The Newfoundlanders, led by an English officer, Lieutenant-Colonel Hadow, were not the first to leave their trenches at the opening of the Somme offensive. They had heard the early waves had not been successful, but when they were commanded to advance to the German front line it was a direct order and they had to go. Knowing how difficult this would be, Hadow first asked his commander if the German trenches, toward which the Newfoundlanders would be heading, were still held by Germans or whether they had been taken by earlier British attacks. He was told that no one actually knew the answer to the question but that the Newfoundland Battalion would have to go anyway.

For the Newfoundlanders this was particularly difficult because they first had to cross three hundred yards of ground before even reaching the British front line. They then had about the same distance to cross to reach the German front line and that latter crossing was over deadly no man's land. Long before they reached the British front line the Newfoundlanders were already being slaughtered by German machine gunners. They were easy targets because the British had not thought to mount a bombardment that might have at least kept the Germans on their guard.

The Germans simply pointed and fired raking across clear open ground where their bullets could not fail to hit the Newfoundlanders. They concentrated their fire on the 752 men advancing over the open ground less than half a mile away. It was like shooting a flock of sitting ducks, one said later. The task was made even easier because the Newfoundlanders could not cross British barbed wire except in one or two places where there were gaps. As the soldiers grouped together to pass through the wire they were even easier to hit and then, as the dead and wounded piled up, those behind them were slowed down and hit. The men who had organised this mayhem were, of course, safely behind the lines. Is it any wonder that the son of Haig, the man behind the Somme Offensive, became a painter?

The Newfoundlanders refused to give up or seek shelter – incredibly, quite a number made it to no man's land, where they too were cut down. Some half dozen miraculously reached the German held front line, despite the fact that they had travelled six hundred yards in broad daylight in the open and with no support. There they were simply shot.

An injured soldier who'd survived an earlier attack and lay in a shell hole described what he saw: 'On came the Newfoundlanders, a great body of men, but the fire intensified and they were wiped out in front of my eyes. I cursed the Generals for their useless slaughter – they seemed to have no idea what was going on.'

In just forty minutes 91 per cent of the battalion was either killed or injured – six hundred and sixty men and twenty-six officers.

A DEADLY GAME

FRANCE, 1916

Nothing epitomises the fact that the Great War was seen as a sort of game than the story of Captain W.P. Nevill of the 8th East Surreys. Nevill fought and died at the Somme, a battle that will always be synonymous with extraordinary bravery and extraordinary stupidity.

But Nevill was famously determined. Before the great, if ultimately disastrous, push at the Somme he waited more impatiently than most for the fighting to begin, convinced that British pluck would win the day in a war that was right and just. For some part of each day he used to stand on the fire step – that ridge that kept the soldiers above the mud and close, but not too close, to the top of the trench wall and certain death, should they be spotted. Nevill stood, every day, and deliberately shouted the worst insults he could think of at the Germans.

Apart from taunting the Germans his biggest worry was his own men. From their position near Montauban they were to be in the first wave to attack, but they had never seen action before and he had no idea how they would react. Like most of the front line officers Nevill believed the massive bombardment of the German trenches by British guns would have knocked out the enemy machine guns, making it relatively easy for his men to move forward, but you could never be absolutely sure. Then he had a brainwave. During his last period of leave before the big push he bought four footballs, one to be given to the men in each of his four platoons.

Back in the trenches he handed out the balls and announced that he had organised a competition with a prize for the winner. The prize would go to the first platoon to kick its ball into the German front line trenches on the day they went over the top. One soldier wrote on his platoon's football the following words: 'The Great European Cup. The Final. East Surreys v Bavarians. Kick off at Zero Hour'.

Nevill, who was a very brave man, decided that when the time actually came he really ought to get the game going. As the noise of the massive softening up bombardment faded – the signal that the attack was about to begin – he climbed up into the open of no man's land, took a few paces forward and executed the most marvellous, perfect kick. The ball soared high, out towards the German line and Nevill, followed by the men he commanded, followed it.

Within minutes there was no one left to collect the prize; most of Nevill's men lay dead or injured. Nevill himself was one of the first to die.

INCOMPETENT CHRÉTIEN

FRANCE, 1916

One of World War One's most important military positions, Fort Douaumont at Verdun, was captured by a single German soldier after an act of supreme incompetence by French General Chrétien. More than 22 million shells were fired at the fifteen forts, including Douaumont, along the line with no effect whatsoever. It was the absentmindedness of one man that was to do what all that ordnance failed to achieve.

Before the disaster of its capture Fort Douaumont was said to be absolutely impregnable – this was assumed because the fort stood behind a line of formidable obstacles. There were two fields of barbed wire no less than thirty feet deep along with close-packed spiked railings, razor-sharp and more than eight feet high. The railings stood behind the barbed wire fields and were separated from the fort by a twenty-four foot deep ditch. The fort itself consisted of a low concrete bunker some two hundred yards long, fitted with regularly spaced loopholes for machine gun fire, and a series of gun turrets. It was also protected by two layers of concrete more than eighteen feet thick with nearly twenty feet of solid earth packed on top. To an outside observer the fort really did look utterly unassailable.

The fort was continuously manned but now and then those who peered from the loopholes and manned the turret guns were changed. When it came to Chrétien's turn he was told to occupy the fort and defend it to the death. But in a moment of madness that he must have cursed for the rest of his life – he was due to go on leave and his mind was clearly on the comforts of home – Chrétien set off without remembering to pass on the order to his men to occupy the fort.

As luck would have it, a German offensive was planned in the next few days and the fort – without Chrétien's reinforcements – had just over fifty gunners, which was far lower than a full complement. The German attack began and with the low number of gunners in the fort it was far easier than it should have been for the German soldiers to cross the wire, the spikes and finally, the ditch. A small party of Germans reached the walls of the fort and crept around, looking for some way to get in. Eventually they formed themselves into a human pyramid and Sergeant Kunze – who was to achieve a certain limited fame for his exploits – found himself at the top of the pile and close enough to a loophole to squeeze in.

Kunze found the corridors deserted until, turning a corner, he came across a group of French soldiers who were completely unarmed. They were so astonished, they surrendered immediately and Kunze locked them in a spare room. He then went to the officer's mess and ate breakfast before allowing his fellow soldiers in so that the rest of the French could be rounded up.

ULTIMATE SACRIFICE

FRANCE, 1916

Every now and then an act of heroism defies all belief. One example is that of Private Billy McFadzean of the 14th Battalion the Royal Irish Rifles.

On 1 July 1916 McFadzean was based in a front line trench near Thiepval Wood, France. It was a quiet day with no enemy action. A box of bombs was being routinely opened prior to distribution among the men. Somehow, as the box was man-handled by several soldiers, it slipped down the side of the trench and fell among a large concentration of men, perhaps as many as a dozen.

Immediately one of the soldiers shouted that two safety pins had fallen out of two of the bombs. The soldiers stood stunned for what seemed like an eternity, but was probably just a second or two. Then, before anyone else could move, Private McFadzean leapt forward and threw himself on top of the box of bombs that almost in that instant exploded. He was killed– in fact he was blown to pieces – but only one other soldier was injured, and only slightly. Private McFadzean was a bomber who knew that, not only would the two bombs without their safety catches ignite, but that in exploding they would ignite all the others and this would almost certainly kill all the men in the immediate vicinity. He must have known he was effectively committing suicide, but as his citation for a posthumous VC put it, 'he knew the danger and deliberately gave his life for his comrades'.

SOMME MISTAKE

FRANCE, 1916

From almost every conceivable viewpoint the first Battle of the Somme must rank as one of the strangest battles in the history of warfare – certainly, it was the bloodiest offensive of the Great War. It came to represent the ultimate futility of battle, inspired some of the greatest poems in the English language and led to a complete change in the way ordinary soldiers could be treated. Before this battle ordinary British and other soldiers had a duty to die for their country without question. But so great was the incompetence of Haig – the aristocratic figure behind the Somme offensive – that soldiers thereafter could no longer be treated as cannon fodder, which explains why today questions are asked in Parliament when a single British soldier dies in action.

The difficulty with the Somme was that the Germans were very secure in their positions when the British and French launched their attack across a twenty-one-mile front north of the Somme River. For a week before the men went over the top a massive artillery bombardment had continued almost non-stop, the idea being to soften up the German defensive positions. What the British commanders didn't know was that the huge bombardment did almost nothing to damage the German positions because the Germans had dug deep concrete-lined bunkers that were almost immune to the barrage.

When the tens of thousands of British and French troops got up out of their trenches – in that immortal phrase they were going over the top – they were easy targets for the German

150

heavy machine guns. They were simply cut down and one infantrymen later remembered how, burdened down with Mills bombs and a full kit as well as his rifle, he and his fellow soldiers were told to proceed in an orderly line toward the German positions and not to run!

By the end of the first day – 1 July – British losses amounted to twenty thousand dead and more than thirty-seven thousand injured. There was a total of 57,450 casualties, Haig's great achievement being to create a new record for the greatest number of losses ever sustained by the British Army in a single day.

Over the months that followed the Somme Offensive became an increasingly pointless and costly exercise. When autumn came rain turned the battlefield into a sea of mud and despite huge losses, the allies had advanced just a few miles. In November Haig called off the attack. As a member of the establishment, he was never criticised, at least not at the time, for a battle that was at best incompetent, at worst seriously negligent. It has been estimated that total casualties for the Somme Offensive were six hundred and fifty thousand Germans, one hundred and ninety-five thousand French, and four hundred and twenty thousand British.

HOOK, LINE AND BOMB BLAST

FRANCE, 1916

Despite all the stories of the horrors of the Great War – the mud and slime of the trenches, the waste of young lives, the fear of death – the over-riding memory of many of those who survived was of something far more prosaic: boredom.

Boredom seems to have sapped the morale at least as much as howitzers, 5.9s and mustard gas. Keeping boredom at bay became a fulltime job for many soldiers. They invented games, kept pets and sang songs, but at least one soldier decided that, whatever the difficulties of the trenches, he was going fishing.

Like many rivers in Northern France before the carnage began the Ancre had been a very good trout stream and a young English officer who had done several tours of duty in the area knew it. Before the war as a child he had visited the area with his parents. He was already a keen angler and had spent hours leaning over a bridge parapet, staring down into the crystal water where, every now and then, he saw the dark torpedo of a trout as it drifted in and out of the weed beds. On those childhood visits he had been unable to fish but with the war on, it was unlikely he thought that a bailiff would turn up if he could get a couple of hours fishing on the river.

He had taken the precaution, when packing for France, of taking a light travel rod, a box of flies and an old reel. War was important, he thought, but so was fishing and besides, these few items of tackle hardly took up any room in his belongings. After one of the worst nights of shelling in his sector the young soldier looked at the sky and thought, 'This is the day!' It was true that the weather was perfect, being mid May and warm with just the lightest breeze. After such a noisy night it was also unlikely the Germans would do much during that day and he would hardly be missed for an hour or two.

Luckily he was in one of the rear trenches and it was easy to dig out his few items of tackle and set off for the river that was just a few hundred yards away. Shells had landed all along the banks and the once lush riverside was dark, muddy and pitted with craters. Here and there the blackened stump of a smashed tree stood as a reminder of what had once been a pleasant rural scene. Now it looked like a barren moonscape, but the river itself was unchanged. It still flowed clear and sparkling, with dense beds of weeds trailing downstream, concealing numerous trout. It occurred to the young man that the trout fishing was probably better now than it had ever been because the river had almost certainly not been fished at all since hostilities began. Undisturbed by fishermen the trout had probably become less wary and there were almost certainly far more of them.

The young man quickly set up his rod and began to cast. He noticed a rise under the far bank, but his cast fell short. Soldiering had taken up so much of his time in the past few years that he was rusty. He cursed his luck – that rise had almost certainly been produced by a good trout. Still he carried on, but few fish were rising and none within range. He looked at his watch and with a pang realised he had been away from his men for nearly two hours. The time had flown but there was not a fish in the bag.

He stopped fishing and simply watched the river for a few moments. Then, as he was about to begin the process of taking down his rod, he noticed a small, but steady rise about halfway across the river: an easy cast, even for him. Out went the line and – more by luck than judgement – the fly fell gently and perfectly just a little upstream of the rising fish. The fly sailed down the stream, there was a splash and the soldier had hooked his fish. But in the very moment he began to play his hard-won trout he heard the unmistakable whine of an approaching shell.

He couldn't believe it. The morning had been absolutely

without incident until now. What should he do? He knew he ought to throw down his rod and take cover, but he could not bear to lose this fish so – against all the rules – he simply stood and continued to play his fish. A moment later he felt himself flying through the air, tumbling, disorientated and covered with water and soil. For a moment or two he lost consciousness and then tried to struggle to his feet. By a miracle he did not seem to be injured but there was no sign of his rod and, of course, his trout had long since vanished.

Sadly he was never to fish the Ancre again. Two weeks after his narrow escape he was killed by a single bullet from a German sniper.

ARAB REVOLT

SOUTH ARABIA, 1916

One of the oddest and most extraordinary soldiers of the past century was the literary hero T.E. Lawrence, or Lawrence of Arabia (1888–1935), as he was to become known.

Lawrence had fought in World War One and, while serving as British Liaison officer during the Arab Revolt (1916–18), he organised a highly unorthodox military operation with a small group of Arabs. He led a raid on the Hejaz railway that isolated the city of Medina, now in Saudia Arabia, and forced the Turks, who were fighting on the side of the Germans, to divert twenty-five thousand troops. This was, by any standards, an extraordinary military coup and one that opened the way for General Allenby's successful offensive of 1918.

Lawrence's activities only became the stuff of legend when an American journalist called Lowell Thomas toured Britain and the Empire giving a sell-out slide-show about his achievements in the Middle East. The romantic image of Lawrence in the desert became fixed forever in the public imagination and from it grew the legend of 'Lawrence of Arabia'.

But Lawrence was a curious mix of bravery and reclusiveness, a man who in many ways loathed his reputation and the adulation it brought him. He was also accused of being a fantasist and over the years there were claims that his successes in the desert had been wildly exaggerated. However, the release of secret papers in the UK in the 1960s and 70s revealed that Lawrence's role in the desert had indeed been extraordinary and pivotal.

Despite his role as romantic hero Lawrence really did hate his fame and all the publicity it brought him. He had few friends, but was very close to George Bernard Shaw's wife, Charlotte, and to Shaw himself. Shaw used to crack jokes about the Public Shaw (himself) meeting the Private Shaw – i.e. Lawrence after the latter chose to enlist in the RAF in 1922 as an anonymous aircraftsman under the name 'Shaw'.

Lawrence hated the idea of being remembered as a war hero. As he wrote to a friend, he wanted to be commemorated as a man of letters, not a man of action. In fact, the huge success of *Seven Pillars of Wisdom*, his book about his time in the desert, has ensured that, to some extent, he got his wish: he will always be remembered both as a man of action and as a literary figure of importance. He died in a motorcycle accident near his home in Cloud's Hill, Dorset in 1935.

TRENCH PHEASANT

FRANCE, 1916

It's a little known fact that throughout World War One all along the line of the trenches in Normandy and Flanders the British obsession with sport – that is shooting, fishing and hunting – continued unabated. There was, of course, a class distinction: it was the officers, not the men, who set out after the rabbit, hares and partridges that had flourished during the years in which men had killed each other rather than them. And, as rations were short – and boring when not – for the British, the chance of a roasted hare or partridge was irresistible.

But, of course, in an environment where bullets and shells from the German trenches were never far away a day's rabbit or partridge shooting had to be carefully organised. Lieutenant Galwey Foley described a day in 1916 when he heard a few pheasants crowing somewhere behind the front line trenches. He decided to have a go for them, but knowing that German snipers were eternally vigilant as well as equipped with highly sophisticated telescopic sights, he decided that a careful strategy was essential if he were to bag the birds without being himself bagged by the Germans. Galwey Foley had hunted pheasants and other birds in and around the trenches many times before so he knew the ropes – the trick was to stalk your birds by dashing from shell hole to shell hole. This sounds more dangerous than it perhaps was: Germans would always be watching but each dash between a shell hole, just so long as it was a dash, would not give the German sniper, however good he was, the chance to get a mark on the pheasant hunter.

157

So Galwey Foley set off at a crouching dash in pursuit of his pheasants. He tripped and fell a couple of times but no shots rang out from the other side. Soon, within sight of the pheasants, he took careful aim and bagged one with his rifle before stuffing it inside his coat and crawling back to his trench for breakfast.

Partridges were particularly plentiful over the trenches but very difficult to hit with the single bullet from a rifle. In letters home Galwey Foley complained again and again that he was sorely in need of a shotgun for these birds, but it is doubtful if the army would have looked kindly on a request for a twelve-bore. He was particularly intrigued by a party of about fourteen partridges that flew over the same part of the British lines every morning before settling among the corpses and mud of no man's land for the rest of the day. In the evening the party would then fly back over British lines, presumably to feed on some abandoned field of wheat somewhere in the rear.

One morning, just before 'stand down', Galwey Foley heard the unmistakable honk of a skein of geese coming from behind the British trenches. The birds soon appeared and headed towards the German lines. In the hope of bringing one down he shouted at the men on the British firing step to give the birds rapid fire. This was done, but the birds passed unscathed. As they reached the German trenches the birds were greeted by a similar fusillade, but with the same result.

On the morning that Galwey Foley heard the geese he saw a pigeon alight on a blackened stump of a tree some sixty yards to the rear of the German lines. Immediately there was a massive fusillade from the German gunners, so loud that many British soldiers thought an attack had begun. In fact, the Germans, at least a couple of dozen of them, were determined to get that pigeon – and not just for the fun of it. Rations were as short for the Germans as the British, and they wanted to eat that bird. In fact, they hit the bird and all that day and into the next night the British kept a sniper with his rifle trained on and near the dead bird hoping that a German, eager for a little pigeon pie, would try to retrieve it. One man leapt up out of the German trenches but after a few bullets whipped up the ground around his feet, he dived for cover and that was the end of that.

Mornings in the trenches for Galwey Foley were devoted to shooting rats with his revolver for the rats – which had never had so much food as they ate the bodies of the dead – were as big as cats. On one memorable day he saw an army cat turn a corner in the trench and come face to face with a huge rat. For a few seconds the two animals stared at each other and then the cat fled!

A SACRED FLAME

FRANCE, 1917

On the Western Front the winter of 1916–17 was deadly. The villages and farms round about had been scavenged for every bit of firewood – rafters, floorboards, furniture, window frames – everything had been ripped out or ripped up to provide fires for the freezing men at the front. But inevitably the fuel ran out, or at least became more and more difficult to find.

Private Briggs, a young man who could neither read nor write, was nonetheless the best and most intelligent scrounger on the Western Front. His regiment guarded him like their best-loved mascot and one day, when the soldiers could stand the cold no longer, Briggs was sent out with a large cart and told to get absolutely anything he could that had even the remotest chance of burning.

He set off for a village called Colincamp, where every house had been reduced to a pile of rubble – why he went there no one ever knew but some instinct must have drawn him. The walls of the church still stood and Briggs investigated the interior like a trained bloodhound. All around was devastation and everything that could be burned had been so already. High up in a wall was a series of niches, each containing a large stone painted statue of a saint. There were a couple of dozen at least, but plaster and stone could not be made to burn. Briggs was stumped but some deep instinct made him prod one of the saints with a long pole; it didn't sound or feel like stone or marble, or plaster. Briggs knocked one down and discovered that the statues were all carved wood. It was the matter of a few moments to bring each statue crashing out of the niche where it had stood for centuries.

An hour later, cheers greeted Briggs as he returned to his battery's position – the saints were chopped into firewood and for that day at least the men were warm.

THE LAST BRITISH ARMY CAVALRY CHARGE

PALESTINE, 1917

World War One was, in many ways, the first modern war but also the last war in which ancient methods still had a place. Aircraft were used, along with heavy machine guns, iron-clad warships and unheard-of amounts of high explosive. Yet amid this vast industrial war, romantic elements high up in British command insisted that something as apparently outmoded as a cavalry charge could still turn the tide of particular battles, if not of the war itself.

This bizarre idea led to what is now generally accepted to be the last British Army Cavalry charge in history. It occurred at the Battle of El Mughar, near Jerusalem, on 13 November 1917 and, amazingly, it was an overwhelming success. The Buckinghamshire Hussars, accompanied by the Dorset and Berkshire Yeomanry Regiments, completely overran a Turkish position, taking hundreds of prisoners.

TRENCH TEA

FRANCE, 1917

The writer Robert Graves, who served as an officer in the Royal Welsh Fusiliers and survived some of the worst horrors of the Western Front, described in his memoirs – *Goodbye To All That* – the ingenious way in which officers in the trenches ensured they had enough hot water to make their tea:

> Our machine-gun crew boil their water by firing off belt after belt of ammunition at no particular target, just generally spraying the German line. After several pounds' worth of ammunition has been used, the water in the guns – which are water-cooled – begins to boil. They say they make German ration and carrying parties behind the line pay for their early morning cup of tea. But the real charge will be on income tax after the war.

FINAL SHOTS

FRANCE, 1918

Right up to the final command to cease fire forever, soldiers on the Western Front continued to fight with the doggedness that characterised what became known as the War for Civilisation. In one or two places along the trenches the fighting didn't even stop at 11 a.m. on 11 November 1918, the exact moment when hostilities were supposed to end. A captain on the British side later wrote:

> At 11.15 it was found necessary to end the days of a Hun machine gunner on our front, who insisted on continuing to shoot. The armistice was in force but what else could we do? Perhaps his watch was wrong but he was probably the last German killed in the war – a most unlucky individual!

SYNCHRONISED PROPELLER

GERMANY, 1918

When aeroplanes were first used in warfare during the 1914–18 conflict they had a major drawback. Bombs could be thrown out by pilot or observer (as the second man was then called) because they could be lobbed out sideways before disappearing into the slipstream and down on to the heads of the enemy. But for really effective use the pilot had to be able to fire in the direction in which he was travelling, but that meant firing a machine gun (or whatever) through the propeller that was mounted immediately in front of the pilot. Early experimenters thought the bullets would travel so fast that they would not hit the spinning propeller; in practice they smashed it to pieces. What was to be done?

Roland Garros, a Frenchman, tried to solve the problem by covering the early wooden propellers with steel. This worked after a fashion but pilots were always in danger of being caught by a ricochet and besides, it was wasteful and inefficient with half the bullets clattering off the propeller in all directions.

The German aircraft engineer Anthony Fokker came up with a better idea: his ingenious answer was to create a synchronised machine gun that shot through the blades by firing precisely in sequence with the propeller itself. The bullets only left the gun when there was a gap in the rotating propeller in front.

That was a relatively sensible invention but it was based on a much madder idea that had been tried a decade or so earlier. An edition of *The Strand* magazine for 1901 mentions a device issued experimentally by Army snipers. This consisted of a wind-up whirring fan with metal blades. When the sniper wanted to peep out from cover to see what the enemy was up to, he would wind up his bullet-stopping fan until it was going at a terrific speed and then, placing it in front of his head and chest, he stepped out. He could see through the whirring blades but if an enemy sniper shot at him, the theory was that the enemy's bullet would be harmlessly deflected. When the sniper with the fan wanted to shoot, he would momentarily stop the blades whirring, shoot quickly and then start them up again.

HEAD SHOT

AMERICA, 1918

Albert Pratt deserves to be better remembered. We know very little about him, but Mr Pratt – an American – was a passionate inventor who came up with dozens of devices to help defeat the Germans in World War One.

One of the most outlandish of these was the gun helmet. A conical hat with peaks fore and aft, the gun helmet had a large bore barrel protruding from the front with a metal sighting device descending from it. Roughly six inches long, the barrel was rifled (grooved internally) to increase accuracy and it was fired by an ingenious air-pipe that doubled as a chinstrap. When the soldier wearing the hat wanted to fire, he blew into his chinstrap; the air travelled up the chinstrap (a narrow flexible pipe) and expanded a rubber bulb inside the hat. As this expanded, it pressed on a trigger that fired the gun. Gases escaping from the gunpowder were used to re-cock the gun for the next shot.

The great advantage of the shooting hat was that it allowed the soldier to fire from the head and simultaneously from the hip with his more conventional rifle. Better still, the hat didn't encumber the soldier as a conventional second firearm would. What's more, it was fairly accurate: the soldier aimed the sighting device (a bit like a short metal calibrated ruler dangling from the front peak of the hat) until a particular mark was lined up on the target and then a quick puff down the tube. In theory, at least, another enemy soldier was out of the action.

The shooting hat is a perfect example, however, of how inventors sometimes let an idea run away with them without looking at some of the more obvious drawbacks. As soon as the shooting hat was tried on a few soldiers, it was realised that the noise of each shot, combined with the recoil, quickly gave the soldiers terrible headaches, as well making them dizzy and, after a while, completely disorientated. For Albert Pratt it was back to the drawing board.

SIGNING THE PEACE

FRANCE, 1918

Over the past one hundred and fifty years and more, children have no doubt been occasionally conceived in railway carriages. Women quite frequently give birth on trains and, sadly, the elderly have been known to depart this world while on a journey on the iron road. Many other momentous events have taken place on trains, from murders to christenings, séances to marriages. But perhaps the most momentous event ever recorded in a railway carriage occurred in 1918.

The carriage still exists and to this day it stands on a sector of what was the Western Front during World War One. Long removed from active service, the carriage is, in appearance, just an ordinary one, typical of the design used by the French Railway Service in the years up to and after the Great War. But within it was signed the Armistice that stilled the millions of guns and rifles that, for more than four years, had levied their toll of death over a thousand-mile front.

Few places have the significance of this simple carriage, where the document was signed that brought peace to a grief-stricken Europe.

EDDIE RICKENBACKER

FRANCE, 1918

To become a war hero you need luck; to become a war hero and a war legend you need luck and time, which is why it is all the more extraordinary that a World War One serviceman became the greatest hero of the war in just six months.

Captain Eddie Rickenbacker was able in that short time to shoot down more enemy planes than any other American airman. Rickenbacker scored a staggering twenty-six successful hits; he downed twenty-two aeroplanes and four balloons, and did it at a time when military aircraft were primitive, to say the least.

Rickenbacker was addicted to speed and adventure. Born in Columbus, Ohio in 1890, he was driven by the desire for excitement and danger. At thirteen he left school and, while still in his teens, he became an extremely successful racing driver. In 1916, his last year of racing, he won sixty thousand dollars in prize money, an extraordinary sum by the standards of the time.

With his passion for speed and machines, Rickenbacker joined up almost as soon as America entered the war in 1917, but he discovered that pilots had to have a university degree and be under twenty-five. At the time he was twenty-seven and had no further education of any kind. Undaunted, he joined General Pershing's staff as a sergeant driver, eventually persuading Billy Mitchell – the colonel for whom he drove – that he should be allowed to enter training to learn to fly. Rickenbacker joined the 94th Aero Squadron and by 1918 he was in the air.

It's easy to forget now how quickly World War One pilots were expected to fly. After beginning basic training the fledgling airman could be considered competent in weeks, or a month or two at most. Rickenbacker flew his first mission against the enemy on 14 April 1918. In no time at all he was knocking enemy aircraft out of the air at the rate of one a week. His successes so impressed his superiors that he was recommended for the Medal of Honor, but it took more than a dozen years for this to be approved.

Clearly Rickenbacker had an extraordinary and particularly fearless personality; his efforts for the War Department during World War Two are a perfect example of this. He was appointed as a troubleshooter but in 1942, on his way from Hawaii to Australia, his plane was forced to ditch in the ocean. He immediately took command of his fellow airmen as they drifted on makeshift rafts for almost a month.

One man died before they were rescued but it is generally agreed that Rickenbacker's indomitable will kept the others alive through their ordeal. He died in 1973 aged eighty-three.

THE BRAVEST MAN WHO NEVER FIRED A SHOT

FRANCE, 1918

World War One seems to have produced more stories of extraordinary bravery than almost any other conflict, yet one of the bravest of all men to take part never fired a shot during his whole tour of duty. Lance Corporal William Coltman, who served with the North Staffordshire regiment, won the highest military honour of all – the Victoria Cross – but then added a bar to it, as well as a Distinguished Conduct Medal and a bar to that. Finally, he won the Military medal.

How did he do it? The answer is that he had one of World War One's most dangerous jobs: he was a stretcher-bearer and if life expectancy was short for the ordinary soldier, it was even shorter for the stretcher-bearers. Despite these appalling odds, Lance Corporal Coltman walked out many times into no man's land under the most ferocious hail of fire from the enemy in order to attend to the wounded and, where possible, bring them back again.

In many cases Coltman had to carry the wounded back himself. Despite the danger he repeatedly exposed himself to the worst the Germans could throw at him. He is the most decorated non-commissioned officer of the whole of the Great War. His VC was awarded for a particular and very specific act of bravery: on 3 October 1918 he volunteered to go out and help the wounded on Mannequin Hill. Despite enemy fire, he went alone and dressed casualties' wounds and, where possible, carried them back to the British position.

172

HAILE INTRIGUING

ABYSINNIA, 1936

Though he may be the spiritual leader of the world's Rastafarians, the late Emperor Haile Selassie had some very odd ideas about mobilising his forces. In 1936 he issued the following Mobilisation Order to the whole country:

> Everyone will now be mobilised and all boys old enough to carry a spear will be sent to Addis Ababa. Married men will take their wives to carry food and to cook. Those without wives will take a woman without a husband. Woman with small babies need not go. The blind, those who cannot walk, or for any reason cannot carry a spear, are exempted. Any one found at home after receipt of this order will be hanged.

FLYING BOAT VILLAGE

AFRICA, 1939

When war broke over Europe, a party of British aircraft engineers was probably among the Englishmen most removed from the conflict that engulfed much of the rest of the world. They were living in huts of planks and thatch on the banks of a remote river in the heart of Central Africa, working away at the hull of a flying boat that lay damaged on the swampy riverbank.

She was the Imperial Airways flying boat Corsair. In March 1939, homeward bound from Durban, she had been forced off course over the Belgian Congo by exceptionally bad weather. Running short of fuel, the captain saw beneath him a small patch of fairly straight water. He managed to land here, but before he could bring the plane to a standstill, she collided with a muddy bank, smashed a huge hole in her hull and sank in a few feet of water. No one was hurt and the mail was completely salvaged by cutting a hole in the top of the hull. The real difficulty was to repair the plane in this remote spot with almost no equipment or materials and get her into the air again and back to Britain, where she was needed for the war effort.

The lake on which the plane was marooned was at Faraje on the river Dangu and the nearest native village was a dozen and more miles away. The solution was to fly out a group of engineers to the nearest airstrip some two hundred miles away; they then had to trek across swamp and thick bush for days to reach the stricken plane. Once there, they had to work in an atmosphere almost as humid as it was hot, constructing a rudimentary dry dock around Corsair's hull, slipping a cradle

174

under her and, with the help of scores of locals, hauling her on ropes to firm ground. They repaired her hull and her roof and launched her again, ready for take-off.

But the take-off presented huge problems. The stretch of river, swollen as it was by the rainy season, was still far too narrow and short, and halfway along its length it took a dangerous bend. Locals were employed to cut down all the trees and rushes along both banks to allow passage for Corsair's wings. A large stake was then driven into the bank and the tail of the flying boat tied to it. Thus secured, her engines were started and revved to full power; when they were roaring, the tie-rope was slipped and she sped at full throttle over the water. She swerved a little at the bend and the captain realised she wasn't going to make it. He cut the engines and she slowed down on the water but crashed into a huge, half-submerged rock. With another huge hole in her hull, the engineers realised months of work had gone for nothing; the whole weary process had to be started again.

She was hauled on to firm ground once more, the hull repaired a second time. By now the War was reaching its most dangerous phase and it was vital to get Corsair back to Britain to help. But the dry season had started, the river had shrunk and there would not be enough water for another take-off attempt for several months. Captain J. C. Kelly Rogers, who had then taken charge of the salvage operations, decided that sooner than wait for rain, he would build a dam clear across the river Dangu and create an artificial lake. It may seem astonishing now that all this effort should be made to rescue one plane but, in the early years of the war, every available plane was needed and flying boats like Corsair were extremely valuable.

The men built a village by the riverside to house local workers and cut a road through the swamp to the site of the proposed dam. They hauled timber from more than thirty miles away, drove a double-buttressed palisade across the river-bed and filled the hollows with stones and mud cut from anthills. At last the water had risen sufficiently far up the depth-board they had planted in the middle of the river and all the submerged rocks had been marked; they were ready for take-off. Once again Corsair's tail was tied to a large stake ashore to restrain her until the engines had reached full power. Captain Rogers took her controls and through the early morning mist Corsair was at last lifted from the patch of water on which she'd lain for nine months. They circled once to dip a salute to the river Dangu and brought her back to her war job on the Empire routes. She went on to fly more than half a million miles, carrying hundreds of tonnes of vital supplies over the war routes.

In Central Africa there is still today a memento of those nine months of toil more than half a century ago. At Faraje, on the Dangu River, the mud village built for the local labourers is still called Corsairville.

WAXED MOUSTACHES

FRANCE, 1940

The ease with which the Germans over-ran France in 1940 is usually attributed to France's lack of military preparedness, but recent research suggests that this is simply not true: France had more guns and equipment than the Germans, so how can their extraordinary defeat be explained? The answer, bizarrely enough, is the telephone, for at least one historian believes that France could have mobilised its army if it had realised that, 'the telephone had been invented'.

The Germans executed what was known as Plan Yellow (or *Vabanquespiel* – 'going-for-broke') and despite every convincing argument, French generals simply refused to react quickly to overwhelming evidence that the real German attack was in the Ardennes and the fake attack would come in Belgium, not vice versa. As a result of this elementary blunder, the war was lost in the five days, 10–14 May 1940.

There is little doubt that the old soldiers who formed the French general staff were like rabbits caught in the headlights of an oncoming car. They did nothing, but perhaps this is not so surprising considering that, despite the existence of the telephone, it still took forty-eight hours for instructions from headquarters to reach field commands. It really was as if the telephone had not been invented. Even the German generals were astonished at the uselessness of the French: one is reported to have said that the French had lost all sense – they could easily have stopped the German advance but were, 'too busy worrying about their honour and the quality of the wax on their moustaches'.

More prosaically, it is probably true that French leaders – like Britain's own Neville Chamberlain – simply could not believe that Hitler would willingly seek war after the disaster of the 1914–18 conflict.

EXTRAVAGANT WINSTON

ENGLAND, 1940

At least privately, almost all military commanders have a tendency to despise other military commanders. The problem with great military commanders is that they have huge egos and tend to be either over-sensitive to criticism, or vain beyond belief. Most commanders in the field seemed to view Churchill as little more than a blusterer who made all the right noises – though they weren't even really agreed about that – but militarily was almost an incompetent.

Sir James Marshall-Cornwall remembered a bizarre meeting with Churchill in 1940. He was invited to dinner at Chequers, the Prime Minister's country house. Marshall-Cornwall was given no information about why he was commanded to attend the dinner, merely being told that a car would pick him up and take him there and that was that. Duly arrived at Chequers, he changed for dinner and sat down with the Prime Minister and others at about eight. Marshall-Cornwall was on the Prime Minister's right and Churchill's scientific adviser Frederick Lindemann came next. Mrs Churchill was also there, along with Duncan Sandys and his wife, the Military Secretary to the War Cabinet Pug Ismay, Jack Dill, Chief of the Imperial General Staff (CIGS), and Lord Beaverbrook, the newspaper baron.

Churchill was in a lighthearted mood, Marshall-Cornwall later reported – almost hysterically so. He quizzed Marshall-Cornwall about the men he commanded and was told that he was trying to stop his commanders having a defensive attitude. 'This must be changed,' he said, 'to a hitting not sitting attitude'. Churchill was delighted with this and told Marshall-Cornwall that he assumed his men were ready for the field. Marshall-Cornwall answered that they were not ready, simply because they lacked equipment and needed another two months' training. Outraged, Churchill pointed to a sheaf of stained and torn papers that he yanked out of his pocket. The papers revealed, he said, that Marshall-Cornwall's troops had been fully equipped and Churchill was again furious when Marshall-Cornwall pointed out that the orders for equipment were correct, but that very little of it had actually arrived. By now Churchill was hopping mad and threw his papers across the table.

An uncomfortable silence followed until Churchill asked Professor Lindemann if he had any news. The Professor pulled out a Mills bomb and began to complain about how it was made – twelve different components were involved and each had to be made separately. It was a bad, time-consuming process, he said, and he had invented a new way to reduce the number of parts and increase the explosive charge of the bomb. The PM's gloomy mood suddenly changed to one of elation and he shouted, 'Splendid, splendid!'

Chief of the Imperial General Staff Jack Dill was horrified and tried to explain that contracts for tens of thousands of Mills bombs had already been placed in America and elsewhere, but the Prime Minister would have none of it and completely ignored him. Beaverbrook, who knew Churchill's crackpot way of running things simply played up to the great man's expectations when asked for his news. He dashed out of the room, returning a few moments later to say that production of Hurricane aircraft had been dramatically increased. It wasn't true – or at least not strictly true – since a temporary increase had been caused by cannibalising halfmade machines and reducing the numbers of bombers being made but Churchill, as Beaverbrook knew, just wanted good news, not the truth.

CATNAPPING

AMERICA, 1941

The British love of animals can be seen throughout the history of warfare – British regiments have animal mascots, dogs and pigeons and other animals have helped in innumerable conflicts and ships' cats have been around for centuries. Perhaps the most famous ship's cat of all came to public attention in the oddest way after one of the most decisive military meetings of World War Two.

It was August 1941 and Winston Churchill sailed to meet US President Franklin Roosevelt aboard the battleship, HMS Prince of Wales. With America still not in the war and Britain struggling almost alone against the Germans, the meeting was pivotal: if Churchill could persuade Roosevelt to fund the Russian war effort, the Eastern Front might drain German resources and manpower.

Roosevelt was aboard the cruiser Augusta and the two ships met at Placentia Bay, Newfoundland. As Churchill stepped off his ship, the Prince of Wales, the ship's cat suddenly appeared and looked as if it was intending to accompany him aboard the American ship, which caused a great deal of amusement for both Churchill and the officers and crew of the HMS Prince of Wales.

After three days of talks Churchill succeeded in his aim and America agreed a massive funding programme for Russia, as well as more merchant ships to bring bombers and tanks to Britain, and an escort of five destroyers and a cruiser for every North Atlantic convoy. Churchill and Roosevelt also signed the

Atlantic Charter – one of the earliest commitments to the idea that we should all 'respect the rights of all peoples to choose the form of government under which they live'.

But what of the ship's cat? Well, it was considered to have brought great good luck to the negotiations and promptly renamed 'Churchill'.

CIVILIAN HERO

ENGLAND, 1941

During the Battle of Britain Norman Tunna, a Great Western railwayman, was awarded one of Britain's highest awards for an act of extraordinary bravery. But this wasn't bravery on the battlefield: it was bravery on the railway.

It was the night of the first big Blitz on Merseyside. On one huge dock area one hundred and forty men of the Great Western Railway were soon to spend the night battling with the help of outside fire services to save the docks, the ships and their huge stores of cotton, food and munitions.

Throughout the long night in the thick of the fires was shunter Norman Tunna. It all began at 7.30 in the evening when the huge dock area and its scores of railway lines were crowded with wagons and locomotives; shunting engines were going to and fro, trains were being taken apart and then re-made, goods discharging and loading. With no warning, suddenly through the clear evening sky came the enemy planes, flying low. The trains and wagons on the dockyard were sitting targets and among them were dozens of freight wagons loaded with high explosive shells of all sizes, waiting to be transferred to barges and ships.

Other wagons were packed with tins of petrol and aircraft fuel, flares, daylight bombs, cordite fuses . . . Here and there tarpaulins covered huge depth charges, the most deadly and destructive of all the loads carried by train during the war. The first bombs the incoming planes dropped were incendiaries: they landed with a tearing sound, then crackled and popped

183

like huge fireworks. The railway men had been drilled to get into their shelters at the first sign of an attack and this they had done. But once the bombs began to fall there was a rush to get out of the shelters. Each man, as he came out, picked up one of the sandbags that had been left round the entrance to the shelter and ran in the direction of the fires, now blazing all over the place. Despite the fires and the bombs that continued to rain down, the railway men could be seen dodging in and out of the railway wagons, kicking incendiaries clear.

Then word came through that one of the biggest storage sheds had been hit by incendiaries. Firemen were working on the roof of the shed where huge panes of glass were cracking and exploding, but despite the heat and the danger the railway men rushed into the shed to see if they could get the trains and wagons clear. By now the blaze from the shed was lighting up the whole dock and the light from the fire was drawing more planes and more bombs. But amidst the raining bombs, the fires and the explosions, the railway men kept working calmly. They seemed to have no thought of danger or personal risk, either on this or on the many nights during which the blitz was to continue.

Then someone realised that a huge ammunition train was up against the side of the blazing shed. It could go up any minute, killing all the men and destroying what was left of the vital railhead. The shedmaster needed shunters but the work was so dangerous, he knew he would have to ask for volunteers. Norman Tunna was first to volunteer, then came his mate Edwards. They knew that six trucks, each containing thirty massive, high explosive bombs, were in imminent danger. Guided by the light from the fires, the two men reached the wagons. Norman Tunna immediately jumped into one of the trucks and began working under the tarpaulin that covered the wagon.

This wagon held the very biggest bombs, packed in with strips of wood and already they were beginning to burn. The two men decided to try to move the burning truck along the rails until it was under the gantry used to load water on to the engines. Tunna climbed aboard the engine and, with the driver, began backing the train away from the burning shed.

They were well on the way to a safer line when they had to halt the train at a signal-box while Edwards went to get orders to proceed. Tunna walked the length of the train to see that all was in order and now, for the first time, he noticed burning debris dropping from one of the high explosive wagons.

He ran back to the engine, got a bucket of water from the injector-pump and warned the driver not to move. Back again with the water, he scrambled underneath the wagon and then threw the water upwards. This put the fire out from under the wagon, but Tunna knew there was still fire inside, under the wagon sheet. To quench this, he ran to another signal box for further bucket of water and a stirrup-pump. Tunna recalled what happened next:

I was trying to work the nozzle of the pump under the sheet when Driver Davies and fireman Newns arrived. They'd come in to work for their shift despite the Blitz. Climbing on top of the wagon, I found a small hole in the sheet through which the incendiary had made its way. Seeing that it was burning furiously, I decided to throw the whole thing open.

'I'll lift the sheet if you'll undo the ties,' I shouted to Davies and Newns. I gave a good lift to the sheet as soon as they had loosened it, and the three of us turned it back. Flames and smoke streamed out of the wagon. Looking down, I could see the wood inside burning fast, and the incendiary, still blazing, jammed between two very big bombs. I made a quick grab for the incendiary, but failed to get it out. It was firmly fixed, and the bombs were getting very hot. Sitting on the side of the wagon I shouted for my shunting pole – thinking to jam it between the bombs, lift one and so get the incendiary out.

I got the pole in, by the incendiary, but the bombs were too heavy for me. Davies and Newns at once climbed in, caught hold of the pole and, between them, levered the two bombs apart. Again, I made a grab for the incendiary. This time I had a good hold of it, and threw it away down the line.

That was not quite the end of the truck fire. The wood was still burning and the bombs getting still hotter. So we got the stirrup-pump working and sprayed the bombs and wood until the fire went out. To make matters completely safe we pulled the train under the water column, and gave all the wagons a good soaking.

After putting the ammunition train away safely, Tunna returned to the main fire and continued helping to get other trains out of the area. At daybreak the raid ended. Without his fearless action the ammunition wagon would have certainly exploded, causing untold damage and huge loss of life. He was subsequently awarded the George Cross.

WRONG NUMBER

ENGLAND, 1941

Like most great leaders Churchill had his eccentricities and one of these was to assume he knew what was going on all the time. On a famous occasion in 1941 he rang the war office – something he did now and then in order to speak to the junior officers, thinking perhaps that he would get the real inside story from them.

It was late at night and he asked to speak to M05, the section dealing with the Middle East. He was put straight through.

'Is that M05?' he asked. The voice at the other end replied in the affirmative. Churchill then asked how the voice thought operations were going in Syria.

'I think it's going very well,' was the reply.

'What about the turning movement the French are trying to make?' was Churchill's rejoinder.

'That seems to be all right,' said the voice.

'Who are you?' asked the Prime Minister.

'Corporal Jones, the Duty Clerk,' was the reply.

The phone went dead.

IN THE NECK

EGYPT, 1941

One of the strangest episodes in the whole of World War Two involved the legendary Major General Orde Charles Wingate, one of the most eccentric – and yet successful – figures in the British army. Having fought an extremely daring and successful campaign behind the Italian lines in Abyssinia in 1941 Wingate went back to Cairo suffering from exhaustion and hallucinations, the latter probably brought on by drugs.

When he tried to get from his hotel room to his doctor he became lost and confused, felt terrified and had to beat a hasty retreat. He felt so confused and ill that he took his temperature and realised it was dangerously high: 104 degrees. Hardly knowing what he was doing, he ferreted around his room until he found his service revolver. He cleaned it, but then realised he had no ammunition and so he took out his big hunting knife went into the bathroom and stabbed himself in the neck.

As he stood there, trying to cut through his own veins and tendons, he apparently thought it might be a good idea to check that his door was locked so, calm as anything, he walked to the door with the knife sticking out of his neck. He locked the door, returned to the mirror, pulled out the knife again and then stuck it in his neck on the other side before fainting from blood loss.

By sheer good luck Colonel Thornhill, a fellow officer staying in the next room, heard the thud as Wingate hit the floor. Thornhill later said that it was the fact that the thump of someone falling over preceded by the door being locked, that aroused his suspicions. Having knocked on Wingate's door and heard nothing, the General rushed downstairs, collected the hotel manager and a spare key and burst into the room just in time to save Wingate, who made a full recovery only to die later in a plane crash.

BIG BANG

ENGLAND, 1942

The novelist Evelyn Waugh, probably the worst soldier in the history of warfare, had a marvellous eye for the absurdities of military life and was adept at recording them – something that would have horrified his superiors. One story he loved to recount, a story that revealed the bizarre incompetence of the military, concerned Lord Glasgow and his plantation of trees.

No 3 Commando, with whom Waugh was serving at the time, were trying to ingratiate themselves with Lord Glasgow, who seems to have been fonder of his trees than of anything else. The senior officers were at lunch with his Lordship. He'd been complaining about a massive old dead tree that couldn't easily be removed from his favourite plantation of young delicate trees, so the Colonel offered to use high explosives and blow the thing out of the ground.

The Colonel instructed his subaltern and the subaltern found the dynamite and placed it under and around the tree. By this time Glasgow had become nervous and asked the Colonel not to bother lest any of his young trees were damaged. The Colonel was reassuring and told Glasgow his men were experts at this sort of thing and could predict precisely where a tree they'd blown down would land – 'We can land it on a sixpence, if we like,' he said.

Glasgow was most impressed and completely reassured. Just to be sure, the Colonel asked his subaltern if there was enough explosive in the tree. The subaltern answered that he had done some very careful calculations and the precise amount required

190

to do the job had been carefully buried in and around the stump. When the Colonel asked exactly how much explosive was being used he was told seventy-five pounds. Worried, he asked if a little more explosive could be added and this was duly done.

Lord Glasgow and the senior officers then trooped out of the dining room to watch the fireworks. Wires were laid, the bomb party moved well back from the offending tree and the charge was ignited. Instead of the massive tree falling in a straight line well away from the young trees – which is what had been planned – the tree and its huge bole rose high into the air and took half an acre of soil and all the young trees with it.

The subaltern confessed to the Colonel that he should have used seven-and-a-half pounds of explosive, not seventy-five pounds. Without a word Glasgow stormed off back towards his castle, but as the grand edifice came into view he saw that every single pane of glass had been broken.

Apparently in great distress, Glasgow ran into the house and hid in – and used – the lavatory. When he flushed the loo, the whole of a massive ancient plaster ceiling fell on his head. Hardly surprisingly Lord Glasgow and No. 3 Commando had very little to do with each other from then on.

POLISH RESCUE

FRANCE, 1942

When the Empire flying-boat Cathay took off from Britain, carrying the Polish General Sikorski and a British liaison officer, she was on one of the oddest missions of World War Two. Her pilot was Captain D. C. T. Bennett, who afterwards transferred to the RAF and became famous for his work with Bomber Command's Path-finders. Their highly secret destination was Biscarosse, where General Sikorski had a rendezvous with the general staff of those formations of the Polish Army still fighting in France.

At about midday they landed on the sea off Biscarosse. A dinghy was put over the side and Sikorski went ashore. Bennett had explained to the General and to his own superiors that the risks of delaying departure longer than a few hours were enormous, but the General said he would not be ready to leave before five o'clock the following morning. Bennett was therefore faced with the huge problem of concealing for seventeen hours a large, unarmed flying-boat on exposed waters liable to enemy bombardment at any moment, towards the shores of which enemy troops were rapidly advancing.

Before long, just as Bennett suspected, the air bombardment of the area began. Afraid that Cathay might be sunk, he taxied her along the coast for six miles and ran her lightly aground on a sandy beach under cover of some trees, turning her violently as he did so, in order that she might come to rest facing open water. The crew stayed there all that afternoon with the sound of gunfire and explosions growing ever nearer. One or two crewmen went ashore later that day and were fired on in the surrounding woods. When they telephoned some French villagers nearby with the thought of getting more provisions, they were warned to keep away as two German tanks and some motorcyclists had just gone down the street. They returned to the flying-boat and sat on board, listening to a distant rumble of tanks on the move. Just before nightfall Bennett started the engines, pulled Cathay off the beach and taxied her back to her original moorings. They stayed there all night, the crew taking it in turns to keep watch sitting on the huge plane's wings, but there were no incidents other than the rumble of German armour, which now sounded ominously close by.

Just before five o'clock in the morning General Sikorski returned, bringing with him his daughter and other officers of the Polish general staff. Cathay took off as quickly as possible, but as she became airborne her crew realised how close they'd come to disaster. They were surrounded by German tanks on the landward side and the Polish officers had to be stationed at the windows of the flying-boat ready to open fire on any enemy aircraft with whatever weapons they possessed. One or two enemy fighters did intercept them, but sheered off, probably because of the Cathay's vague similarity to the formidable RAF Sunderlands.

At one point it seemed that Cathay was in big trouble, but astonishingly Bennett managed to take refuge in a thick pall of black smoke drifting from some oil tankers burning on the French coast and to shake off the pursuers. While still flying in this smoke, he calculated an estimated time of arrival at a point on the south coast of Britain, which proved to be spot-on.

Cathay brought the Polish staff safely to Britain, but having survived this close encounter, Sikorkski was to die in mysterious circumstances in 1943 when his plane took off from Gibraltar and immediately crashed into the sea. Rumours surrounding the circumstances of the crash – including a suspicion that he was murdered, possibly even by the British – have never completely gone away.

ANTI-CHURCHILL

ENGLAND, 1942

For decades Churchill's reputation has been unassailable: Churchill the war hero, Churchill the saviour of the nation – he may have been eccentric, dogmatic, bloody minded even, but he was a man who made sense of the maxim: 'Cometh the moment, cometh the man'.

Before the Great War Churchill's contemporaries viewed him in a very different light. He was deemed unreliable after changing political parties when he failed to get his way and he was considered a dangerous maverick, unreliable, inconsistent and unfit for high office, or indeed at one time for any office at all. Yet when World War Two began he seemed to be the man above all others with the personal qualities needed to lead Britain.

In an extraordinary outburst that he committed to print, Field Marshal Lord Alanbrooke was utterly contemptuous of the Great War leader. Chief of the Imperial General Staff for most of World War Two, Alanbrooke advised Montgomery and Churchill and, as Chairman of the Chiefs of Staff Committee, he was a central figure on the British side in conferences with Roosevelt and Stalin and at Casablanca, Teheran, Malta and elsewhere.

Even allowing for a personality clash – Churchill and Alanbrooke certainly did not get on – there may be something in his damning verdict on Sir Winston. He wrote:

He knows no details, has only got half the picture in his mind, talks absurdities and makes my blood boil to listen

194

to his nonsense . . . And the wonderful thing is that three quarters of the population of the world imagine Winston Churchill is one of the great strategists of history, a second Marlborough, and the other quarter have no conception what a public menace he is.

VERSE AND WORSE

INDIA, 1942

Military men are not renowned for their love of literature. Soldiering and verse seem to produce a literary cast of mind and a slight disaffection from the aims of the soldier. But there are exceptions – Field Marshall Lord Wavell is a case in point and his love of verse led to some wonderfully mad confusions.

While Wavell was stationed in India the threat from the Japanese became intense and all officers were instructed to make sure they had regular revolver practice. Why anyone should think that revolver practice would prevent a Japanese incursion, no one seems to know but there it is.

Wavell's military assistant, Peter Coats, later recalled how Wavell called him to his room one evening. The Field Marshall's desk was littered with a huge mess of papers and books – the drawers open and turned out, filing cabinets clearly ransacked. Wavell looked terribly worried, distressed even, and on seeing Cook immediately said to him:

'Peter, I can't find my Browning. Did you borrow it?'

Cook spent more than an hour searching high and low for the Field Marshall's revolver before discovering that what he was actually looking for was his copy of Robert Browning's collected poetry!

TANK-TOP VC

FRANCE, 1943

It has been said that in order to win a Victoria Cross – the UK's highest military honour – you have to act in a way that is almost certain to lead to your death. But of course in most cases death isn't courted directly: it happens as a consequence of some reckless act that reveals a soldier's complete disregard for his own safety. But in at least one instance the winner of the VC seemed absolutely determined to die, yet against all the odds not only did he survive, but survived completely unscathed.

Infantryman Corporal Nanjit Singh was moving forward behind a line of tanks towards a river crossing on the Marne when heavy fire knocked out several tanks and the advance ground to a halt. A small group of men, including Singh, was sent out on reconnaissance mission but just a few hundred yards into a stretch of open ground they came under sustained heavy machine gun fire and three of the group were badly injured. The rest beat a hasty retreat.

It was still broad daylight but Corporal Singh volunteered to try to bring the injured men in. Under a hail of bullets he successfully rescued the first of the injured men before running out again and bringing in the second. It seemed impossible that he had not been hit. Thinking he would need to adopt slightly different tactics to get to the last injured man, Singh climbed on to a tank and had it driven slowly out into the patch of open ground where the injured man lay. Singh sat cross-legged in full view of the enemy on the top of the tank with his arms folded and his head held high while a hail of bullets was directed at him. Meanwhile, two orderlies were able to dash out and rescue the third man.

The enemy, no doubt astonished by the Corporal's antics, barely noticed the orderlies concentrating their fire instead on the presumed lunatic on the tank. Despite the rain of bullets Corporal Singh returned to his lines without a scratch.

THE MADDEST SOLDIER
IN THE ARMY

BURMA, 1943

Orde Wingate did not believe in bathing – instead he brushed his body daily or cleaned it with a toothbrush. He ate raw onions in large quantities believing, as did the Roman soldiers who were instructed to eat them before battle, that they were good for valour. Wingate also hated to be seen in a smart uniform or to have to kowtow to important visitors. It was said that he kept a filthy suit in reserve and only put it on when dignitaries arrived in Khartoum, where he was stationed in the early part of World War Two. But Wingate's abilities as a soldier were not in doubt for Winston Churchill thought he was pretty much a military genius who could do no wrong.

Wingate was also a loner with a fierce temper and a single-mindedness that terrified many of those with whom he came in contact. He wore beef dripping in his hair and was continually rude to, or dismissive of, his superiors. Despite this, he organised a brilliant guerrilla campaign in Ethiopia against the Italians.

Wingate was born in 1903, into a family of Plymouth brethren – a sect that, even today refuse to use computers or watch television, or have zips on their trousers. Fanatically religious as a child, strangely he also loved hunting and was always in the most dangerous places when out in pursuit of foxes. Later, when he tried hunting big game, he used to charge at any animal foolish enough to attempt to charge at him. At the last minute he would dodge to one side and fire as the animal passed by.

During the most difficult years of his Africa campaign Wingate regularly wandered into the desert alone, with neither food nor water, just to see how long he could stand it. He took a copy of the Bible and nothing else with him. Fiercely pro-Arab, he switched sides and became a devoted Zionist, who fought against the Arabs during their rebellion in 1937. He was awarded a DSO and was a familiar sight in a huge pith helmet, wandering around singing hymns in Hebrew.

Eventually his enthusiasm for the Jewish cause led to his recall. The British authorities thought he had become unhinged, but Wingate refused to be beaten and wrote a personal letter setting out the rights of his case to King George VI!

Wingate's most extraordinary exploit has to be the occasion on which, having been sent to Ethiopia, he persuaded fourteen thousand Italian troops to surrender by tricking them into thinking they were surrounded by artillery. And how did he do it? He had one artillery piece dragged quickly from place to place round the Italians, fired, then moved, then fired again. The Italians naturally assumed they were surrounded and promptly gave up. Sent back to Cairo – for insubordination and indiscipline – Wingate tried to cut his own throat, but was saved by a colleague.

By now the army had just about had enough of him and he was due to be shipped to an obscure posting when Field-Marshal Wavell decided that Wingate was just the man to help him fight the Japanese in Burma. Suddenly Wingate was in his element. In eighteen months he went from Major to acting Major-General and organised long range penetration groups behind Japanese lines, disrupting enemy communications and generally creating havoc. Despite his successes he lost almost one-third of his three thousand men – known as the 'Chindits', a corruption of the Burmese word for lion – in the first half of 1943.

But the Chindits' became legendary and when Churchill asked Wingate to dinner at 10 Downing Street he was so impressed that he immediately invited him to meet the Allied Chiefs of Staff in Canada. The Americans loved Wingate and he returned to Burma with renewed confidence. In keeping with his unorthodox methods, to save time he forbade any of his men to shave.

A few weeks later he was killed when his plane flew into a mountain.

DONKEY

ALBANIA, 1943

In most conflicts soldiers attract animal mascots and some men become so fond of them they will do almost anything to protect them. Whether a ship's cat, a dog found wandering in a trench or a captured songbird, an animal seems to be a reminder of life back home away from the conflict.

One of the most bizarre incidents concerning an animal involved British Liaison officer David Smiley in Albania in 1943. In a country still, in many ways, in the Dark Ages, transport was extremely difficult to come by, so Smiley bought himself a mule for five shillings and christened her 'Fanny'. Smiley became completely besotted by his new companion, who was friendly, well behaved and loyal.

For six months Fanny carried Smiley everywhere but the time came for the officer to return to England on leave. He left Fanny with a friend with strict instructions that she was to be looked after well. After a few weeks away he sent a telegram to Alan Hare, with whom he'd left Fanny, asking how she was.

By now it was winter and Smiley knew that with food shortages it would not be easy for Hare and his fellow soldiers, but he was horrified by the telegraphed reply from Hare, which simply said, 'Have eaten Fanny'.

SHARP-SHOOTING WOMEN

RUSSIA, 1943

It's a little known fact that the Russians, used no doubt to the idea of women miners and factory workers, had one of the most effective female fighting forces in World War Two: they were an elite band of women sharp-shooters. Generally speaking, one of their instructors later said, they were more deadly than their male counterparts, a claim borne out by the fact that in 1943 alone it is estimated that in Russia roughly one thousand female snipers accounted for more than twelve hundred kills. During that year just a single woman sniper – Senior Sergeant Roza Shanina – was awarded a string of battle honours for a total of 54 kills.

LANDING PRACTICE

ENGLAND, 1944

During the run up to the Normandy Invasions in 1944 training sessions were organised in the South West of England under conditions of great secrecy. The exercises were scheduled at Start Bay in Devon and involved units ultimately headed for Utah Beach. More than twenty-five thousand men and nearly three thousand vehicles took part but, incredibly, the decision was taken to allow the men to use live ammunition despite the fact that this was a simply a training exercise.

A bizarre and foolish decision quickly turned to farce when, during the mock assualt landing, US defenders failed to realise they had live ammunition. They began to fire not over the heads of the attacking 4th Infantry Division and 1st Engineers, but at them! A number of soldiers were very badly injured although, according to the official record, none were killed.

A day later as landing craft raced towards the beaches in the second phase of the mock battle they were attacked by real German E-boats. In the confusion the landing craft commanders assumed the attacks were part of the exercises and did nothing to defend themselves: two assault craft were sunk and another badly damaged. More than seven hundred US soldiers died, but there was a cover-up and it was not until 1954 that the full facts of the disastrous training session entered the public domain.

DOGS OF WAR

RUSSIA, 1944

During World War Two the Germans, British and Japanese all trained dogs to help with the war effort. The different levels of humanity in each country can best be judged by the fact that the Russians and the Japanese used half-starved dogs that were sent out carrying bombs: effectively these were dog suicide bombers. But the British were too fond of them even to contemplate such an idea.

The Russians probably trained more dogs than anyone and some fifty thousand were recruited or bred specifically for the purpose before and during the war. They were used to attack the enemy or to discover the enemy's position, but mostly to rescue injured soldiers, who in the dreadful Russian winter were likely to die from exposure rather than their wounds if they were not rescued quickly.

Dogs were much faster through the snow than horses or vehicles and when they found a man they were trained to lie next to him to try to keep him warm till help arrived. An Alsation called Bob received a bravery award for saving some sixteen wounded men in this way: the men had crawled into shell holes and ditches to escape the worst of the driven snow and were subsequently found and kept warm by Bob.

The Russians awarded a number of special medals to their dogs. These included the Order of Bagdan Khmelnitsky, the Order of the Red Star and the Order of Alexander Nevsky.

Alsations, or German Shepherds, were most often used for rescue work while pure white Samoyeds were excellent for winter attacks. They would pull Russian marksmen (dressed in white) on sleds towards the enemy lines: they could move silently and were almost invisible until it was too late for the enemy to react.

Russian suicide dogs were kept half-starved and trained to search for food under tanks. When enemy tanks were in sight they would be released and had special armour-busting bombs attached to their backs. They would run towards the enemy tanks then dash about underneath them until a special pressure trigger exploded the bomb, which cut through the underside of the tank.

There are many examples of the success of these suicide anti-tank dogs. At Izyum, for example, they are said to have been so effective that as soon as the Germans heard barking they turned their tanks round and fled. However, it was not all plain sailing. According to some reports the dogs sometimes got confused and ran back under their own tanks and destroyed them.

The Japanese were probably the least effective in using dogs – they knew so little about training them that they thought harsh training methods would work best. In fact the dogs were hopeless simply because they responded more to American gestures of friendliness than to their Japanese masters. In 1944 the Japanese tried using small dogs to run towards the American lines before running back to the Japanese. The Japanese would time the dogs' journey out and back in order to gain some idea of the enemy's position, but they had forgotten that the Americans could easily turn this to their advantage: they simply followed the dogs to find out where the Japanese were!

ONE MAN'S WAR

NORTH AFRICA, 1944

Caught alone in the open desert by two Italian fighter planes, the English soldier did not react as one might have expected, for during a military career of startling and consistent eccentricity Vladimir Peniakoff had made a point of doing things in his own inimitable way.

He'd been reading his copy of Milton's epic poem 'Paradise Lost' while enjoying the morning sun under a spindly acacia tree when he first heard the angry buzz of the planes. Though he could have run for cover, instead he decided to hold his ground. He quietly pocketed his book and then peeked from behind his thin tree as the first plane came in low to attack.

Peniakoff dodged out from behind the tree, wiggled his hips at the approaching plane, waved at the pilot and then dodged back behind the thin tree trunk as a hail of bullets threw showers of sand into the air all around him. The next plane made its approach and he began a bizarre dance that involved thumbing his nose at the pilot and then waving at him when his bullets failed to find their target. This continued until the Italian pilots, weary of wasting time and bullets, gave up and headed for home. Peniakoff returned to 'Paradise Lost' as if nothing had happened. This was just the latest in a long line of bizarre antics.

Born in Belgium of Russian parents Peniakoff had first come to England as a child. After Cambridge he became a pacifist, who worked in an army gas factory during World War One. During the 1920s he drove round the Egyptian desert in a battered old car he nicknamed 'The Pisspot'. When it fell to pieces he cannibalised it to make a large pushchair in which he carried all his possessions, including his copy of 'Paradise Lost'.

He was forty-two when World War Two began, but immediately joined up. Impatient with conventional warfare he decided to set up a Commando Unit in North Africa to attack German fuel dumps. With just twenty-three men, Popski's Private Army – the nickname arose because no one could pronounce 'Peniakoff' – was the smallest unit in the British Army, but it was also one of the most effective.

Peniakoff refused to have any officers and saluting was forbidden. He himself dressed like a tramp but his reports to the Eighth Army from behind enemy lines were said to be invaluable. His greatest success came when he captured a heavily fortified German lookout tower simply by waiting for one of the guards to step outside for a pee. As soon as the man came out, Peniakoff nipped through the door the soldier had left open and in less than a minute the tower was secure and he had taken five prisoners.

CHANCE MEETING

GERMANY, 1945

With millions of men and machines on the move it is not really that surprising that extraordinary meetings occur during warfare, along with remarkable coincidences and bizarre encounters.

One of the strangest of these was recorded by Douglas Sutherland, who was in a tank at the head of an infantry column. Suddenly the tank ahead of him found itself engaged in a fierce battle. Sutherland's tank was just missed by a bazooka and he was lucky: had it struck home it would almost certainly have pierced the shell of the tank and killed the occupants. As it was, the lead tank fired at the point from which the bazooka had been launched and that was the end of the battle. Having cleared the way, the tanks could move on and allow the infantry to move up behind, which is what duly happened. The tanks settled into cover at the edge of a wood and the tank crews tried to get some sleep.

In the morning the first tank moved a few feet and then the most extraordinary thing happened: a figure rose from underneath the place where the tank track had remained stationary throughout the night. It was a grimy, bedraggled, sodden figure in torn clothes and hat, but it – or rather he – was alone and apparently uninjured.

All that could be made out was the tattered remnants of a German uniform. The grisly, rather pathetic figure raised its hands and then gingerly pointed back to a slit trench in which he'd been trapped by the tank track. Clearly, he'd spent the night tightly wedged in that underground slot barely able to breathe, let alone move.

Sutherland was intrigued as the man who seemed vaguely familiar. He gestured to him to climb up on to the tank. As he reached the top and sat opposite him there was an astonishing moment of recognition: back in the 1930s Sutherland's father had decided his sons should learn German and the best way to do it would be to hire a German tutor. The tutor who had eventually taken the job was called Willie Schiller and the grimy German soldier who'd spent the night under the tank track was Willie Schiller.

The two men hardly said a word to each other but Sutherland gave him a cigarette and a tot of rum and they sat together companionably despite the fact that they were sitting in the centre of a scene of carnage. Another soldier was given the job of escorting Herr Schiller back behind the lines and into captivity, and in recognition of their former friendship Sutherland gave strict commands that Schiller was to get there in one piece.

MISTAKEN IDENTITY

ENGLAND, 1947

H.G. Michelmore used to fish the River Dart at South Hams in Devon. It was an excellent bit of water with plenty of good free-rising trout. However, the beat he fished most regularly was part of an American military firing range and practice battle-ground. Over the years numerous servicemen had been accidentally killed and one day in the late 1940s, fifty or sixty yards from the bank, Michelmore noticed a fresh mound of earth with a white cross at its head. From then on he never passed the place without bowing his head and remembering the poor soldier who had died. He felt so sad about it that he never actually wandered over to view the grave more closely. Having served in the Great War himself Michelmore was acutely sensitive to the memory of any fallen comrade, particularly in a case like this where a young man's life had been pointlessly wasted.

After some time Michelmore found he was fishing more often in the South Hams area. He felt a great affinity with the soldier lying in his grave just a few yards from the bank and he began to salute quietly and unobtrusively whenever he passed the spot.

Then, one bright summer morning, Michelmore's wife decided to accompany her husband on his regular fishing trip to South Hams. This was a rare event indeed, but Michelmore was delighted to have company. As they walked together along the riverbank enjoying the warm breeze and the crisp, early sun he explained the story of the dead soldier and how deeply it had

211

affected him. He said that each time he passed the soldier's grave he felt strangely moved by the young man's end, but comforted himself with the thought that at least one man had not forgotten.

When they reached the place Michelmore pointed through the trees to the barely visible white cross. His wife asked him if he was going to fish, but Michelmore said he did not feel comfortable fishing in the place despite the fact that it was one of the best parts of the river.

'I think you might be able to from now on,' said his wife in a quiet voice.

'What on earth do you mean?' asked Michelmore.

Without a word Mrs Michelmore set off through the undergrowth towards the grave. A few minutes later she returned with what looked like a barely suppressed grin on her face. Her husband thought the smirk was rather unwarranted, but he said nothing.

'Well, what's his name?' He eventually asked.

'Well,' replied his wife, 'he appears to have died in 1944 and his name was officer's latrine!'

From that day on Michelmore avoided the spot, but for very different reasons.

COLD WAR TESTS

ENGLAND, 1955

Few democratic governments use their own subjects in scientific tests that are likely to lead to the death of the subject. That sort of thing is normally left to dictatorships, but during the Cold War the British government seems to have lost control of a series of these activities.

When documents were released under the Freedom of Information Act in the 1990s, police discovered strong evidence that Ministry of Defence officials had lied to British servicemen in the 1950s to get them to take part in dangerous experiments. Volunteers were told they were being given new drugs designed to cure the common cold – in fact, they were illegally given highly toxic chemicals, about which little was known.

The police investigation was triggered by retired serviceman Gordon Bell, who gave evidence about what had been done to him. Despite more than four decades having passed since the tests the police decided to pass their evidence to the Director of Public Prosecutions. They wanted to know if it was sufficient to mount a prosecution of those still alive who conducted the tests and to try to get compensation for victims still alive. The tests were carried out at the top secret MOD research station at Porton Down near Salisbury, which is still used to carry out highly secret weapons and chemical trials.

But detectives investigating claims from the 1950s discovered that it wasn't just a matter of one or two individuals being used for highly dangerous tests. In fact, thousands of military personnel had been exposed to mustard gas, various types of nerve gas and other highly dangerous chemicals in what has been described as the longest-running series of chemical warfare trials on humans in history.

Mr Bell's evidence has been corroborated by other independent evidence. A police statement said that it was, 'apparent that a criminal offence of administering a noxious substance, contrary to section 24 of the Offices of the Person Act 1861, had been committed' against him by Porton scientists. The result for the government was growing calls for a full and independent inquiry into why a government department was conducting highly dangerous military experiments on its own people. One critic said it was as bad as the Nazi experiments on prisoners of war.

CHAMPAGNE CHARLIES

EGYPT, 1956

Bizarrely, during the Suez Crisis the army didn't have enough tank transporters to move its tanks so Pickfords (the removals company) made a small fortune doing it for them. Further difficulties were experienced when the army realised it couldn't get Pickfords' employees to do the long hours soldiers were routinely expected to work. Transporting the tanks and other equipment using the civilian vehicles took almost twice as long as it would have taken using army personnel, which added to the confusion and delay.

But if the tanks and other vital equipment took weeks longer than they should have done to reach the South Coast ports, more absurdities were in store when the heavily laden ships finally reached Port Said. One huge truck took forever to move down the ramp from a cargo ship: in fact, its progress was so slow that a senior staff officer approached the driver and began to berate him for delaying the whole operation. By this time the lorry was stuck fast and the problem was clear – it was so overloaded that the suspension had failed, crushed under the huge weight of whatever the massive lorry contained.

Furious, the staff officer asked the driver what he was doing. A lofty voice drifted down from the cab and explained that the lorry contained the officers' mess silver and champagne!

DISAPPEARING FROGMAN

ENGLAND, 1956

British attempts at espionage reached a low point with the still unexplained disappearance of Royal Navy frogman Lionel Crabbe in 1956. Crabbe, who joined the Navy in 1941, had seen service in Gibraltar, where he worked in a mine and bomb disposal unit removing limpet mines from the hulls of Allied ships. At first he just disarmed the mines brought up by British divers, but the more glamorous, if highly dangerous part of the work, led him to retrain as a diver.

His efforts under water so impressed his superiors that he was eventually awarded a George Medal and promoted to Lieutenant Commander. In 1943 he became Principal Diving Officer for Northern Italy and was later appointed OBE. By this time his prowess in the water had earned him the nickname 'Buster', after the American Olympic swimmer, Buster Crabbe.

After the war Crabbe served in Palestine before finally being demobbed in 1947. But the lure of the sea proved too much, and he continued to dive for private companies before returning to the Navy. He dived to investigate sunken Royal Navy submarines and, on one occasion, went down to investigate a Soviet ship, the Sverdlow.

By 1955 Crabbe was in his late 40s and persuaded to retire. A year later MI6 brought him out of retirement to investigate the Soviet cruiser Ordkhonikidze, which was lying at anchor in Portsmouth Harbour after bringing Russian premier, Nikita Krushchev, to Britain.

On 19 April 1956, in conditions of enormous secrecy, Crabbe dived into Portsmouth Harbour and vanished forever. His disappearance remains one of the great mysteries of the Cold War, not least because although a body was later found, it had been deliberately mutilated by having the head, hands and feet removed.

An attempt to cover up the whole botched operation was immediately begun. Crabbe's companion took all his belongings from the hotel, where they were staying and even tore out a page in the hotel register, where they had signed in. MI6 and the Admiralty lied about what had happened, telling newspapers that Crabbe had vanished in Stokes Bay. But the Soviets caused huge embarrassment when they announced that they had spotted a frogman near their ship in Portsmouth Harbour.

British newspapers got on to the story and simply would not drop it. They suggested the Soviets had taken Crabbe to the Soviet Union. Prime Minister Anthony Eden asked MI6 Director General John Sinclair to resign, which he did, and then – in 1957 – a body in a frogman's suit was found. Its head, both hands and feet had been cut off, making it very difficult to identify. An inquest returned an open verdict, but the coroner said he was satisfied that the body was that of Lionel Crabbe.

The story produced, as such stories will, a vast number of conspiracy theories. Some said Crabbe had been killed by a secret Soviet underwater weapon, while others insisted he had been taken to Russia and brainwashed to work for the Soviet Union. Or that he was a Soviet Navy commander with a new identity and that MI6 had asked him to pretend to defect so he could become a double agent . . . But a Soviet Naval Intelligence Officer, who later defected to Israel, said a marksman on the Ordkhonikidze had noticed Crabbe in the water and shot him. If the simplest explanation is likely to be the most true in matters like this, that is probably what happened. The removal of the hands, feet and head would have been a crude attempt to make identification for the British authorities extremely difficult.

PIGS MAY FLY

CUBA, 1963

It is a truism of warfare that even the best-laid military plans tend to go awry. That is true even if the country behind the plans is one of the mightiest nations on earth. The famous Bay of Pigs invasion of Cuba that was backed and fomented by the world's most powerful nation is a classic example of absolutely extraordinary incompetence and bungling. Even John F. Kennedy, US President at the time, admitted in papers only released much later that he really should have resigned over the fiasco.

The source of the Bay of Pigs farce was America's largely irrational obsession with communism. One can understand the Americans' fear of a huge, powerful communist nation but, at the point at which they became obsessed with newly socialist Cuba, it really was only a small, relatively insignificant nation, albeit one that was rather close to the American mainland.

The real difficulty was that in the years after the Cuban revolution the rich and well-educated – more than a quarter of a million, in fact – left Cuba. Castro's revolution helped the poor enormously, which is why he enjoyed their overwhelming support, but the better-off felt hugely disadvantaged and left in their droves for America, where they plotted their return and the ousting of Castro.

The poor might have been better off under Castro, but they did not get the elections he promised. Like all dictators he came up with specious arguments about why elections would actually make life more difficult for everyone. He claimed, for example, that the national unity created by his leadership would be destroyed by competing political parties in an election. He was also becoming paranoid and anyone who questioned the great leader was sacked or imprisoned while Castro toadies, even when young and stupid, were given jobs in the government for which they had neither the experience nor the ability.

Journalists who criticised Castro were arrested, along with homosexuals and anyone else Castro decided he didn't like. Eventually he behaved more like a petulant pop star than a statesman and was to be found surrounded only by fanatics, who often, quite by chance, were young, good-looking and female.

The Americans were increasingly worried by what was going on and, in March 1960, a top government official, Richard Bissell, drafted a top-secret paper called 'A Program of Covert Action Against the Castro Regime' (code-named JMARC). Bissell was joined by a team of CIA men, who had years earlier worked to oust the then government of Guatemala. The policy centred on creating a Cuban government in exile, a propaganda machine, an armed resistance group in Cuba and a paramilitary force outside Cuba. Bissell wanted Castro removed by force. Eisenhower, the American President in 1960, authorised $13m to pay for JMARC.

As part of the military and tactical offensive against Castro some exceedingly bizarre plans were hatched. These included a scheme to spray a television studio in which Castro was about to appear with a hallucinogenic drug. Another suggestion, and it was a serious one, was to put the drug thallium on Castro's shoes. It was believed by numerous figures in the White House that this would make the hair in his beard fall out. Why that would necessarily discredit him, or force him to resign remains a mystery to this day.

In the end Bissell decided to go for the straightforward assassination of Castro. In September 1960 he met Allen W. Dulles, then director of the Central Intelligence Agency (CIA) and – incredibly – began talks with two top Mafia men, Johnny Roselli and Sam Giancana. The Mafia was offered $150,000 to kill Castro – they were known to be furious with him for closing down their brothels and casinos in Cuba. That meant that if anything went wrong with the assassination attempt the Mafia would be seen to have a motive and official government involvement would not be discovered. The FBI agreed to the plan and the Mafia negotiated a deal where their activities in the States were given a wide berth by the authorities in return for their help.

Kennedy became involved in November 1960. The Mafia plot had come to nothing and he was not impressed by a new invasion plan that involved a seven hundred and fifty man team landing on a beach near the port of Trinidad, on the south coast of Cuba. The CIA thought Trinidad a hotbed of opposition to Castro, and with airborne support and after gathering around them other disaffected Cubans, it was assumed that within a week or so the invasion force would be able to take over the country and depose Castro. Nervous and unconvinced, Kennedy had the plot independently vetted. The invasion was given a thirty per cent chance of success. Sensibly, Kennedy told Bissell to go away and think again. How could seven hundred and fifty men possibly hope to defeat Castro's two hundred thousand strong army even if they did manage to gain some localised support?

Bissell's new plan involved a landing at the Bahia de Cochinos (Bay of Pigs), much closer to the island's capital of Havana than the proposed original landing at Trinidad. CIA director Allan Dulles said later, 'We felt that when the chips were down, when the crisis arose in reality, any action required for success would be authorized rather than permit the enterprise to fail.' Dulles and the others clearly knew that the seven hundred and fifty man invasion would not be a success, but they thought Kennedy would then order a full-scale invasion.

Bissell told Robert Kennedy that plan B, as it were, had a seventy per cent chance of success. Kennedy gave the plan the go-ahead, but insisted that instead of sixteen bombers sent in support only eight were to be used, which made the invasion far less likely to succeed.

B-26 planes duly bombed Cuba's airfields, leaving the country with only eight planes and seven pilots. Two days later five merchant ships carrying one thousand four hundred Cuban exiles arrived at the Bay of Pigs. A second air raid was planned, but Kennedy cancelled it, meaning the invasion would almost certainly fail and that the lives of the invaders would be lost – which is exactly what happened.

On 18 April 1961 Bissell told John Kennedy that the invasion force was trapped on the beaches and encircled by Castro's forces. Bissell asked Kennedy to send in American forces to save the men, but Kennedy refused. Within three days all the invading troops had been either killed or captured. Kennedy later admitted that the fiasco was his fault, but in a bizarre defence of his actions he is reported to have said, 'In a parliamentary government, I'd have to resign. But in this government I can't, so Dulles and Bissell will have to go.'

Dulles and Bissell duly resigned and a military operation that could have been better organised by a banana republic came to an ignominious end.

TROPHY HUNTER

VIETNAM, 1965

All wars make men less than human and civilised behaviour becomes not the norm but the exception. Even the most mild mannered can become callous torturers under the right conditions. Vietnam seems to have been a particularly brutal war with the Americans increasingly astonished that despite their vastly superior fire-power they simply could not win – or at least they could not win in a manner acceptable to the rest of the world. If they'd dropped a few atomic bombs, no doubt the North Vietnamese would have thrown in the towel, but America's reputation worldwide would have been damaged beyond repair and there was a further risk of Russian retaliation. The result was a long and dreadful, ultimately pointless, war in which the ordinary American soldier was as a much a victim as an aggressor.

Bizarrely, apart from the Americans and the Vietnamese, other countries including Australia contributed soldiers. Two Australian commandos once turned up in an American command post looking very much the worse for wear. They were extremely rough looking, but they had been involved in a pitched battle the day before and still bore the scars. But they were also pleased, as they had managed to get hold of a trophy from one of the North Vietnamese they'd killed. This turned out to be two burned and blackened human ears that the Australian soldier had strung on a wire and was planning to wear around his neck.

FOOTBALL CRAZY

HONDURAS, 1969

The years 1968–69 saw increasing unrest in Honduras as the government struggled with huge economic problems and a series of industrial strikes by vast numbers of key workers.

As the situation worsened the government increasingly blamed the three hundred thousand Salvadorian immigrants in the country. Then a decision to expel from their land anyone who was not Honduran by birth raised tension to fever pitch. Salvadoreans began to leave Honduras by the thousand but they were returning to an already overcrowded and desperately poor country.

In mid 1969, while all this unrest was going on, the Honduran and Salvadorian football teams began a three-game match, which was a qualifier for the World Cup so it was a game that – to football fans at least – mattered a great deal.

The first match produced fights in the crowd; the second, in San Salvador, was much worse. Honduran fans came off worst and their flag was burned outside the ground. Revenge attacks on Salvadorerans became commonplace in the days and weeks that followed the match. The Hondurans seemed to have become unhinged and Salvadoreans began to be killed and as panic set in, the stream of Salvadoreans leaving the country became a flood. On 27 June 1969 Honduras broke off diplomatic relations with El Salvador.

The completely insane 'Soccer War', as it came to be known, began in earnest on 14 July 1969 and has to go down in the history as one of the most stupid wars – two small, poor nations

223

fighting it out because one had insulted the other at a football match. The Salvadoran air force bombed Honduras, the subsequent invasion pushing the Honduran army back over six kilometres. At Nueva Ocotepeque, their momentum spent, the Salvadorean army became bogged down largely because the Hondurans had bombed and damaged the Salvadoreans' oil facilities.

Four days later, when pressure from various international economic groups forced the Salvadoreans into withdrawing their troops, the war was over. Honduras agreed to stop persecuting Salvadoreans living in Honduras and that was that. In fact, though the killing stopped it was to be more than a decade before the two sides finally reached a meaningful peace agreement.

The war had caused the forced expulsion of around one hundred thousand Salvadorans from Honduras; some two thousand people, mostly Honduran civilians, had been killed. Unhappy with both the war and the peace the Hondurans were eager to blame someone so they blamed their military, who fell massively from favour. The real cause of the war, for which the football match had been a flashpoint, was probably the age-old desire to blame the foreigner for the economic ills of the country. At worst, this led – as we know – to the Nazi holocaust.

Like most South American countries both Honduras and El Salvador suffered – and still suffer – from poverty and Catholicism. When El Salvador needed the economic safety valve of its population being able to drift into Honduras all was well, if uneasy. But this meant Honduras had a large, illegal population of workers perceived by the Hondurans as taking too many jobs and using up too many resources – a classic situation that only needed a football match to turn it into war.

ASIAN HITLER

CAMBODIA, 1973

The Cambodian mass murderer Pol Pot – also known as 'Brother Number One' – was one of the world's most extraordinary military leaders, who used his energy and skill to kill more than three million of his own countrymen, including women and children.

Until 1953 Cambodia was a French colony, or Protectorate as the official history books like to put it. A sixteen years' monarchy with Prince Norodom Sihanouk at the helm followed until the war in neighbouring Vietnam destabilised the country and caused an increase in opposition to Sihanouk. When the opposition movement became a serious threat, the royal army crushed it, thereby forcing its members underground. Here, revolution was fomented and eventually the opposition emerged as the Khmer Rouge, the Cambodian communist movement led by Pol Pot – one of the maddest military movements ever to have existed anywhere in the world.

Pot was born in 1925 in Kampong Thum province, north of Phnom Penh. At the age of 21 he joined the Indochinese Communist Party before leaving to study electronics in Paris. He failed his degree, but read Marx and later joined what became known as the 'Paris Student Group' – most of the leaders of the Khmer Rouge were to come from this group. Back in his homeland he became a history and geography teacher, but kept up his enthusiasm for Communism, and in 1960 he took control of the Workers' Party of Kampuchea (WPK).

225

By 1963 Pot was WPK's general secretary, having almost certainly murdered the previous incumbent. He then fell out with the communists in both China and Vietnam and by the mid 1960s his party was known as the 'Khmer Rouge'. By the late 1960s a spell living with a Cambodian Hill tribe convinced the increasingly deranged Pot that everyone should live the simple life, but that meant simply the life as defined by Pol Pot himself.

By 1970 Sihanouk had been ousted and Defence Minister Lon Nol was made premier of the newly proclaimed Khmer Republic, a coup supported by the American CIA. Pot's Khmer Rouge worked against the new republic and by 1973 the Khmer Rouge – now run in an increasingly dictatorial way by Pot – was in control of sixty per cent of Cambodia's territory and twenty-five per cent of its population. In March of 1973, the Khmer Rouge captured the city of Odongk and completely destroyed it, forcing people into the countryside and killing all office workers, teachers and academics.

By April 1975 Phnom Penh had fallen to Pot. The population of over two million was then marched into the countryside at gunpoint and people with no experience of living off the land were simply told to get on with it or starve, and starve they did. Pot announced that time in Cambodia was starting again from Year Zero – all signs of outside influence were to be destroyed in pursuit of the simple rustic life and anyone who disagreed would be killed immediately and without trial. All foreigners were expelled, embassies closed, money abolished. Schools, offices, markets, newspapers, magazines and private property were made illegal – anyone found hankering after any aspect of the past was to be executed. Pot, admittedly not the first insane ruler of a country, thought this was all perfectly reasonable.

Those deemed to be educated and middle-class were executed without trial, which led to a situation where people who had worked in offices or schools would rub their hands on walls and tarmac streets until they bled in order to make it look as if they were manual workers. The whole country was forced out of cities and towns into the countryside, where they starved or were killed by Pot's soldiers, who were told to watch them and execute anyone not pulling their weight, or showing the least sign of opposition.

It is difficult to establish an exact figure, but at a conservative estimate more than two million people were worked or starved to death, or were shot for infringements of the new rules. Most were shot for complaining, not working hard enough, eating too much, wearing jewellery, having sex, getting upset when friends and family were executed. In one torture centre – Tuol Sleng – nearly fifteen thousand men, women and children were tortured to death in three years. At least twenty other centres carried out the same level of killings.

Some two hundred thousand were executed when Pot decided his own troops and members of his party were unreliable. Faction slaughtered faction in a vast, blood-letting frenzy. Eventually Pot named himself prime minister and 'Brother Number One'.

In 1978, horrified at the genocide taking place in their neighbouring country, the Vietnamese invaded Cambodia. Pot and the defeated Khmer Rouge went into the jungle, from where they fought a guerilla war for the next twenty years. By 1980 Pot, still at large, had been sentenced to death by the new Cambodian government. Meanwhile, rapprochement between the Soviet Union and China caused the Soviets to apply pressure on Vietnam to withdraw their forces from Cambodia.

By 1996 the fragmentary remains of the Khmer Rouge were breaking up and in August of that year Ieng Sary, Khmer Rouge 'Brother Number Three', defected to the Cambodian armed forces, naming Pol Pot as the sole instigator of the Khmer Rouge policies of genocide. Pot was eventually arrested by Ta Mok, also known as 'Brother Number Five'. By this time he was ill, but he gave an interview to a journalist in which he said he had done absolutely nothing wrong: a declaration that every dictator in the history of the world would echo. All that he had done, he said, had been for the good of his people and if one or two of his officials had been over-zealous in carrying out their duties . . . well, that was not his fault.

He said: 'My experience was the same as that of my movement. We were new and inexperienced and events kept occurring, one after the other, which we had to deal with. In doing that, we made some mistakes . . . I admit it now and I have admitted it in the notes I have written.'

In 1998 Pol Pot died, probably from heart failure, but he may have been murdered, and was cremated on a pyre of old car tyres.

In August 2001 the Cambodian Government set up a tribunal of local and international judges and prosecutors to try former leaders of the Khmer Rouge for genocide, but the Cambodian government refused to allow the trials to be run on internationally acceptable lines and the United Nations pulled out.

Two Khmer Rouge are still in detention – Ta Mok, the military commander who arrested Pol Pot in 1997, and Kaing Khek Iev, who ran the Tuol Sleng detention centre. They are unlikely ever to stand trial.

NO SURRENDER

PHILIPPINES, 1974

From 1944 until 1972 a Japanese soldier hid in a remote Philippine jungle refusing to surrender because he did not believe that World War Two had really ended.

The story began in 1944 when Lieutenant Hiroo Onoda was sent to the Philippine island of Lubang with strict instructions to continue a guerilla war against Japan's enemies and never, under any circumstances, to surrender. When the war ended less than two years later everyone forgot about Onoda and for the next twenty-eight years he lived wild in the jungle, surviving on coconuts and bananas, and avoiding search parties again and again because he believed they were enemy combatants who were out to kill him.

Onoda's orders had come from Major Yoshimi Taniguchi and Major Takahashi. He was told, 'You are absolutely forbidden to die by your own hand. It may take three years, it may take five, but whatever happens, we'll come back for you. Until then, so long as you have one soldier, you are to continue to lead him. You may have to live on coconuts. If that's the case, live on coconuts! Under no circumstances are you to give up your life voluntarily.'

Onoda's mission was to destroy the airfield on Lubang and the pier at the harbour but, as the Japanese war machine began to crumble, the allies arrived in huge numbers and Onoda retreated to the hills. Gradually his men surrendered or died, but Onoda and four others evaded capture and lived in caves and sometimes in trees, living on any fruit they could find. Occasionally they stole a cow or a goat.

Until the early 1950s there were several cells of Japanese soldiers and each would occasionally attack the search parties sent out to look for them. Other cells were captured or killed while Onoda's continued to fight despite the passing of the years and the utter silence from their superior officers. Even when, in the late 1940s, Onoda found a leaflet saying, 'The war ended on August 15. Come down from the mountains' – he simply assumed it was a trick, a further example of enemy treachery and propaganda. And even when leaflets signed by General Yamashita of the Fourteenth Area Army were dropped on the island Onoda refused to believe them – he simply thought they were fakes because it could not be possible that Japan had lost the war.

But the authorities knew Onoda was there and they continued to try various means to get him to give up. Newspapers were left in the jungle, letters from relatives dropped from aeroplanes. Onoda and his men may have seen them, but clearly they thought treachery was afoot and they stayed stubbornly in the dense jungle covered hills.

Isolated from the rest of the world, the four soldiers thought everyone was the enemy and as the years passed their sense of paranoia increased. Search parties were continually fired on and one or two of those engaged in the search injured. But then things began to change: in 1949 one of Onoda's four men surrendered. In 1954, one of Onoda's three remaining men was killed in a skirmish. For the next twenty years Onoda and his friend Kozuka stayed in the jungle, undetected and rarely seen. By this time they knew the jungle better than anyone and could easily avoid the search parties that still went out occasionally to look for them. Onoda was still convinced that he must remain behind enemy lines in order that the Japanese could eventually regain the island.

In 1972, Kozuka was killed during a clash with a Filipino patrol. Search parties again intensified their search for Onoda, but still he could not be found. Then, in 1974, a Japanese student set off for Lubang and against all the odds managed to make contact with Onoda. He tried to convince him that the war really was over, but Onoda said he could only surrender if ordered in person by Major Taniguchi. Eventually the Major was flown out to Lubang and there, he met Onoda and read the statement of Japanese capitulation. Onoda was astonished that Japan had lost the war. He is reported to have said, 'How could we have been so sloppy as to lose?'

He still had a few bullets and his rifle and, after nearly thirty years of living rough in the jungle, he unloaded his gun, took his pack off and gave up. Over the years Onoda and his men had killed thirty Filipinos, but his story was so extraordinary that he was officially pardoned by the Philippine government.

Back in Japan he was treated to a hero's welcome, but it was all too much and he left for Brazil, where he bought a ranch. In 1996 he returned again to see the island where he had spent the best part of his adult life.

COLLATERAL DAMAGE

IRAN, 1988

The whole issue of civilian deaths in war is fraught with difficulty. During most wars the difficulties of fighting on the ground mean that many civilians lose their lives as a result of being fired at – sometimes in error, sometimes deliberately – but more usually they simply get caught in crossfire.

Highly sophisticated electronic weaponry and extremely sensitive detection equipment makes many feel, erroneously as it happens, that military mistakes on a large scale are a thing of the past. The fact is that any improvements in war-making materials and equipment designed to protect soldiers are more than outweighed by the incredible destructive power of modern military might. If an incident occurs, the chances are that it will be catastrophic.

A good example of this is the almost incomprehensible shooting down of an Iran Airlines airbus during the 1980–88 Iran–Iraq war. The US cruiser Vincennes spotted the airbus and opened fire, mistakenly believing it to be hostile. As a result, nearly three hundred passengers and crew were killed and US–Iranian relations reached an all-time low.

The captain of the US warship was probably extra-sensitive to attack from the air, following an attack a year earlier by an Iraqi airplane on the US ship Stark. In this incident 37 crewmen were killed and the blame laid at the feet of an over-cautious ship's commander. From having acted too late to prevent disaster, US ship commanders went to being over-eager to fire, which explains the downing of the Iraqi airbus.

The Vincennes was equipped with a mass of military radar hardware, including a state-of-the-art system called Aegos, but for all its sophistication it was more suited to attack and certain destruction than to discriminating real from imagined targets.

THE LOVE BOMB

AMERICA, 1991

A research project set up by the United States military in the early 1990s lasted five years and cost more than $5 million. It was designed to look at the possibility of developing an aphrodisiac bomb that could be dropped on enemy troops, infecting them with a chemical that would make them find each other sexually irresistible. One part of the research examined chemicals that would make soldiers feel irresistible to each other. Released under the US Freedom of Information Act the plans were developed by the US Airforce's Wright Laboratory in Dayton, Ohio.

Another line of research carried out by the same team looked at creating bombs that would release extremely offensive smells, including flatulence and faeces. Eventually, this idea was dropped – not because it was scientifically impossible but because, in the words of a US Airforce spokesman, the smell of faecal matter was not considered offensive in many of the theatres of war in which the US military operated!

The idea of a sexual chemical bomb was really tapping into research that suggested the absolutely vital role of pheromones – chemicals carried by all humans – in human sexual behaviour. Newly emerging genetic research also suggested that the right kind of smells could be created but the research into using human scent offensively foundered when it was realised that military discipline and the fear of retribution were always likely to outweigh the effects of attractant chemicals.

234

HIGH FLYERS

AMERICA, 1994

Early aviators simply would not have believed how aviation was to progress during the twentieth century and beyond. It's not just that you can now fly in great comfort from Europe to Australia in a day, nor that aircraft can carry hundreds of passengers at a time over those huge distances. The real advances in the science of aircraft engineering are to be found in military aircraft. Where scientific energy has traditionally concentrated on creating aircraft that remain stable whatever the conditions, military aircraft designers have, in recent years, deliberately tried to introduce inherent instability.

This may sound completely mad but it actually represents the sanest end of aircraft invention. The idea behind the usefulness of instability for flight comes from bird observation. In flight, birds are supremely manoeuvrable because their on-board computers – their brains – allow continual and very rapid adjustments to wind speed and direction. When the bird needs to move very quickly – to jink to avoid a predator or dive to catch prey – its brain allows the normal flight pattern to be disrupted and the bird goes into free fall, or does a dramatic turn. Jumbo jets and other commercial aeroplanes are the complete opposite: they are so stable they respond relatively slowly to the pilot's controls. That's fine for a plane designed to cross the Atlantic in comfort, but military planes are better off in combat if they can go into sudden free fall to avoid an enemy or jink and twist second by second to outmanoeuvre a pursuer. Modern computers make this possible because they can adjust the controls in microseconds to keep the plane on an even keel during normal flight, while allowing the option of sudden chaos when rapid manoeuvres are needed.

However, the use of computers for this sort of thing has led to at least one bizarre invention that is applicable to passenger aircraft: – the paddle-driven aeroplane. At the moment lift for all aircraft except helicopters is provided by large wings. An alternative is to have lots of short wings arranged in the pattern we see on old-fashioned paddle steamers. The mass of wings mean there's plenty of theoretical lift, but until modern computers it would have been impossible to translate the lift from these spinning blades into an overall lift stable enough to keep a large aeroplane in flight.

Of course such a plane has yet to be tested but the patents are there if anyone is feeling brave enough to build a prototype, and computers can at least in theory cope with the huge complications of the physics involved.

STRANGE MEETING

JAPAN, 1998

Eric Lomax was one of hundreds of thousands of Allied prisoners and Thai labourers forced by the Japanese to work on what became known as the 'Railway of Death'. From Thailand to Burma, the line was forced through by the Japanese military using brutally tortured and starved prisoners.

Lomax did something few others have ever done, however. Fifty years after the war had ended and still scarred, mentally and physically, by the treatment he had received – which included torture at the hands of a particular Japanese interpreter – he tried to find the man who had treated him so badly. Incredibly the Japanese interpreter was still alive. Lomax contacted him and they arranged to meet.

They met on a bridge over the 'Railway of Death' and the elderly Japanese simply bowed and asked forgiveness. The two men talked to each other and then parted and although Lomax did not exactly forgive his former torturer, the experience of meeting him seems to have exorcised half a century of anguish – an anguish Lomax found difficult to share with others.

ANIMALS AT WAR

LONDON, 2004

A monument unveiled in London's Park Lane in 2004 is the first ever to recognise the enormous contribution various animals made to Britain's efforts during World Wars One and Two. The monument shows a horse, a dog, two mules and a sad list of the number of animals killed as a result of human aggression. But what makes it so extraordinary is the range of animals it commemorates: apart from horses, dogs and mules, there are pigeons and glowworms, for example.

One historian has said that it was the British love of animals and their inventive relationships with them that made key differences at crucial times to the ability of British forces to win campaign after campaign. Some of the assistance given by animals is so strange as to be almost unbelievable – glowworms, for example, really were used in the Great War to enable soldiers to read their maps at night!

The most fascinating part of this strange monument, however, is the detailed list of some sixty animals each awarded the Dickin Medal since 1943. The Dickin Medal is the animal equivalent of the Victoria Cross, which is given for 'conspicuous gallantry'.

Among the sixty-two recipients of the Dickin Medal are thirty-two pigeons, eighteen dogs, three horses and a cat – all from World War Two. The stories of all these animals are remarkable. Take Winkie, the pigeon that flew more than one hundred miles with her wings badly clogged with oil in order to save a bomber crew that had ditched in the sea. Or Rob, a dog in the parachute regiment, who made more than twenty parachute jumps into Africa on highly dangerous missions with the Special Armed Services.

Then, during the recent war in Iraq, there was Buster, a Springer spaniel who detected a huge cache of arms thereby probably saving the lives of many civilians and soldiers. Also mine detector dog Ricky, who carried on working after receiving head injuries from an explosion. During the Blitz in London dogs like Beauty, Peter, Irma and Jet located survivors buried in buildings destroyed by the Germans' nightly bombing raids.

The inscription on the monument in Park Lane reads, 'Animals In War. This monument is dedicated to all the animals that served and died alongside British and allied forces in wars and campaigns throughout time. They had no choice.'

KITCHEN FIGHTERS

IRAQ, 2005

Modern warfare is as prone to the bizarre as earlier conflicts despite huge improvements in defensive and offensive technologies. War is often a matter of luck and chance, which may explain why those who escape death and injury, even in the worst situations, seem almost to have something supernatural about them.

On 22 March, in one of the worst areas of the Iraqi capital of Baghdad, a United States patrol was attacked by heavily armed insurgents (to use the favourite US–British coalition word). When the attack began, there were just ten US personnel in three trucks. The Iraqi insurgents were well equipped with rocket launchers, machine guns and grenades. One American soldier described the minutes after the attack began as 'a scene of complete pandemonium' with bullets and rockets raining down on them and apparently from every conceivable direction. An objective observer would have said that the ten Americans were doomed.

Sergeant Leigh Ann Hester, who was in the thick of it, said, 'When we first started taking fire, I just looked to the right and saw seven or eight guys shooting back at us – muzzle flashes. You could hear a lot of booms from the rocket-propelled grenades; you could hear bullets hitting metal.' As the convoy continued along the road at least one vehicle took a direct hit from a rocket-propelled grenade and the ten soldiers were forced to get out of their vehicle and fight on the ground. Amazingly, they beat off the insurgents who, by all accounts,

240

completely outnumbered them and the only injuries sustained by the Americans were superficial.

The extraordinary element of luck involved in all this can best be judged by the fact that these American soldiers were not highly trained Green Berets or marines – in fact, they weren't regular soldiers at all. Among the ten were a shoe shop manager, a hotel worker, a printer and several students.

The battle was a reminder that the US Army, the best trained and richest army in the world according to many commentators, is made up of more than forty per cent reserves – in other words, amateur soldiers!